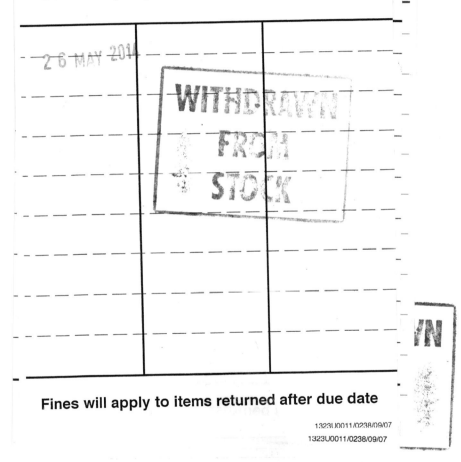

Conduct Disorders in Childhood and Adolescence

Developmental Clinical Psychology and Psychiatry Series

Series Editor: Alan E. Kazdin, Yale University

Recent volumes in this series . . .

Conduct Disorders in Childhood and Adolescence

Second Edition

Alan E. Kazdin

Volume 9
Developmental Clinical Psychology and Psychiatry

 SAGE Publications
International Educational and Professional Publisher
Thousand Oaks   London   New Delhi

For information address:

SAGE Publications, Inc.
2455 Teller Road
Thousand Oaks, California 91320

SAGE Publications Ltd.
6 Bonhill Street
London EC2A 4PU
United Kingdom

SAGE Publications India Pvt. Ltd.
M-32 Market
Greater Kailash I
New Delhi 110 048 India

Printed in the United States of America

Library of Congress Cataloging-in-Publication Data

Kazdin, Alan E.
    Conduct disorders in childhood and adolescence / Alan E. Kazdin. — 2nd. ed.
        p.   cm. — (Developmental clinical psychology and psychiatry; vol. 9)
    Includes bibliographical references and indexes.
    ISBN 0-8039-7180-X (Cased: alk. paper). — ISBN 0-80390-7181-8 (pbk.: alk. paper)
    1. Conduct disorders in children. 2. Conduct disorders in adolescence. I. Title. II. Series: Developmental clinical psychology and psychiatry; v. 9.
    [DNLM: 1. Child behavior disorders. 2. Social behavior disorders— in infancy & childhood. 3. Social behavior disorders—in adolescence. W1 DE997NC v.9 1995 / WS 350.6 K23c 1995]
    RJ506.C65K389 1995
    618.92'89—dc20   95-5295

This book is printed on acid-free paper.

95 96 97 98 99 10 9 8 7 6 5 4 3 2 1

Sage Production Editor: Gillian Dickens

To Eve and her remarkable warmth and élan

CONTENTS

SERIES EDITOR'S INTRODUCTION

Interest in child development and adjustment is by no means new. Yet only recently has the study of children benefited from advances in both clinical and scientific research. Advances in the social and biological sciences, the emergence of disciplines and subdisciplines that focus exclusively on childhood and adolescence, and greater appreciation of the impact of such influences as the family, peers, and school have helped accelerate research on developmental psychopathology. Apart from interest in the study of child development and adjustment for its own sake, the need to address clinical problems of adulthood naturally draws one to investigate precursors in childhood and adolescence.

Within a relatively brief period, the study of psychopathology among children and adolescents has proliferated considerably. Several different professional journals, annual book series, and handbooks devoted entirely to the study of children and adolescents and their adjustment document the proliferation of work in the field. Nevertheless, there is a paucity of resource material that presents information in an authoritative, systematic, and disseminable fashion. There is a need within the field to convey the latest developments and to represent different disciplines, approaches and conceptual views to the topics of childhood and adolescent adjustment and maladjustment.

The Sage Series **Developmental Clinical Psychology and Psychiatry** is designed to serve uniquely several needs of the field. The Series encompasses individual monographs prepared by experts in the fields of clinical child psychology, child psychiatry, child development and related disciplines. The primary focus is on developmental psychopathology, which refers broadly here to the diagnosis, assessment, treatment, and prevention of problems that arise in the period from infancy through adolescence. A working assumption of the Series is that understanding, identifying, and treating problems of youths must draw on multiple disciplines and diverse views within a given discipline.

The task for individual contributors is to present the latest theory and research on various topics, including specific types of dysfunction, diagnostic and treatment approaches, and special problem areas that affect adjustment. Core topics within clinical work are addressed by the Series. The present monograph focuses on conduct disorder and serious antisocial behavior such as aggressive acts, theft, vandalism, setting fires, and related behaviors in children and adolescents. The nature and scope of the problem, as well as its prevalence and costs to society, make antisocial behavior one of the most socially significant mental health problems. The present book integrates current findings on description, diagnosis, assessment, treatment, and prevention of conduct disorder. In addition, new models to approach the investigation and treatment of antisocial behavior are identified to guide future research.

—*Alan E. Kazdin, Ph.D.*

PREFACE

Conduct disorder refers to a clinical problem among children and adolescents that encompasses aggressive acts, theft, vandalism, firesetting, running away, truancy, defying authority, and other behaviors referred to as "antisocial." Many antisocial behaviors, in mild form, emerge over the course of normal development, and hence prove to be of little consequence. Persistent and extreme patterns of these behaviors among children and adolescents reflect a serious clinical problem with broad personal and social impact. These more extreme patterns are delineated here as conduct disorder.

The significance of conduct disorder stems in part from the fact that it constitutes one of the most frequent bases for referral of children and adolescents for psychological and psychiatric treatment. Children with severe antisocial behavior are not only seriously impaired as youths, but also are likely to manifest psychiatric problems, criminal behavior, and social maladjustment when they become adults. The problem does not end when the antisocial youths reach adulthood; as parents, they are likely to pass along antisocial behaviors to their offspring who continue the cycle.

The costs of conduct problems are exorbitant. There are, in addition, the personal costs to the many victims of aggressive, violent, and cruel acts completed by youths with conduct disorder. Such youths are victims themselves given the abuse, neglect, and poor care to which they are often subject. Apart from the personal and often tragic consequences of antisocial behavior, the dysfunction continues as one of the most costly of childhood disorders. These children and adolescents and their families use multiple social services and are in frequent contact with the mental health and criminal justice systems. The lifelong impairment absorbs enormous resources.

The significance of the clinical and social problem that conduct disorder reflects is heightened by the absence of clear solutions. Parents, teachers, and victims of all ages are confronted with youths who engage in severe antisocial acts; policymakers struggle to redress the problem with programs of all sorts. To date, it seems as if little can be recommended to curb the problem; also, it seems that no treatment or prevention program is available or in sufficiently widespread use to have significant impact. Actually, within the past few years significant advances have been made both in treatment and prevention.

This book describes the nature of conduct disorder and what is currently known from research and clinical work. Findings are drawn from such areas as criminology, epidemiology, psychiatry, and psychology. The subject matter brings us to such topics as psychiatric diagnosis, child rearing practices, parent psychopathology, the contributions and interactions of heredity and environment, sex differences in development, psychotherapy research, and others. The book considers core areas of work that occupy current research efforts. These include elaboration of contemporary diagnosis and methods to assess conduct disorder, identification of risk and protective factors that influence the onset of the disorder, the paths and courses of conduct disorder over the life span, and current methods of treating and preventing the dysfunction. The purpose is to provide a comprehensive yet concise view of conduct disorder in children and adolescents and to point to new areas of work. To that end, the book ends by outlining new models for and approaches to critical questions regarding diagnosis and treatment of antisocial youths.

The second edition takes the opportunity to showcase many advances and lines of research that have moved the field forward. Gains have been made in many areas in terms of diagnosing and delineating subtypes of dysfunction and elaborating how early influences unfold leading to conduct problems. Also, within the past few years, the evidence for treatment and prevention has made significant gains. The range of procedures and strength of the evidence in their behalf has increased. In this edition, an effort has been made to elaborate findings in diverse areas that build on the core knowledge of the field regarding the nature of the problem and its impact on the individual and others.

The many influences that shaped this book cannot be fully elaborated, but a few had very special impact during the preparation of this edition. First, the ambience and support of Yale University, in particular the Department of Psychology and Child Study Center, are conducive to the type of work this monograph represents. Stimulating colleagues and students, as well as the clinical staff with whom I work on a daily basis, have been of enormous help and education. Second, interactions with colleagues in the John D. and Catherine T. MacArthur Network on Psychopathology and Development (Chair, Dr. David Kupfer) have shaped much of my thinking about the complexities of developmental psychopathology and their impact on the conceptualization of dysfunction. Finally, the support of a Research Scientist Award (MH00353) and funding to develop treatments for conduct disorder children and their families (MH35408) from the National Institute of Mental Health have been central to my development and understanding of childhood dysfunction. To each of these influences and the many individuals they encompass, I am pleased to acknowledge the support and input.

A. E. K.

1

INTRODUCTION AND NATURE OF THE PROBLEM

Antisocial behaviors include a broad range of activities such as aggressive acts, theft, vandalism, setting fires, lying, truancy, and running away. Although these behaviors are diverse, they often go together. Thus children who are very aggressive are likely to show some of the other antisocial behaviors as well. The behaviors all violate major social rules and expectations; many of them also reflect actions against the environment, including both persons and property.

Many different terms have been applied to denote antisocial behaviors including acting out, externalizing behaviors, conduct disorder or conduct problems, and delinquency. Two of the terms are worth delineating at the outset. For our purposes, *antisocial behavior* will be used to refer broadly to any behaviors that reflect social rule violations, acts against others, or both. Examples include various acts such as fighting, lying, and other behaviors whether or not they are necessarily severe. Such behaviors are evident in clinically referred youths, and they also are seen in varying degrees in most children over the course of normal development.[1]

The term *conduct disorder* will be used to refer to instances when the children or adolescents show a *pattern* of antisocial behavior, when there is *significant impairment* in everyday functioning at home or school, or when the behaviors are *regarded as unmanageable by significant others.* Thus conduct disorder is reserved here for antisocial behavior that is clinically significant and clearly beyond the realm of normal functioning.[2] Clinically severe antisocial behavior is likely to bring a youth into contact with various social agencies. Mental health services (e.g., clinics, hospitals) and the criminal justice system (e.g., police, courts) are the major sources of contact for youths whose behaviors are identified as severe. Within the educational system, special services, teachers, and classes are often provided to manage such children on a daily basis. Even though the behavioral problems that constitute conduct disorder are familiar, it is useful to illustrate the level of severity and the surrounding circumstances that characterize clinically severe levels of impairment.

TWO CASE ILLUSTRATIONS

Greg

Greg is a 10-year-old boy who lives at home with his mother, father, two younger brothers, and a baby sister. He was referred to an outpatient clinic because of his excessive fighting, temper tantrums, and disruptive behavior at home and at school. At home, he argued with his mother, initiated fights with his siblings, took money from his parents, and constantly threatened to set fires when his parents disciplined him. On three separate occasions, he actually had set fires to rugs, bedspreads, and trash in his home. One of these fires led to major damage, costing several thousand dollars. Greg also lied frequently; at school his lying got others into trouble, precipitating frequent fights with peers and denials of any wrongdoing.

Greg was brought to the clinic because his parents felt that he was becoming totally unmanageable. A few incidents in particular were mentioned as unusually dangerous—for example, Greg's attempt to suffocate his 2-year-old brother by holding a pillow over his face. Also, Greg had recently wandered the streets at night and had broken windows of parked cars. Because of some of the older boys with whom he interacted in the neighborhood, the parents were also worried that he would become a "hood." Greg's parents occasionally resorted to severe punishment by using paddles and belts or by locking Greg in his room for 2- to 3-day periods. These punishments appear to have been in response to setting fires in the home.

Several characteristics of Greg's family life are noteworthy. Because Greg's mother and father had worked all of Greg's life, a relative (the maternal grandmother) had primary care responsibility of the children. For the 2 years before Greg was brought for treatment, his father had been employed only sporadically. The father spent much of his time at home sleeping or watching television. The loss of work, income, and lack of his help around the house contributed to increased stress at home. Greg had said that he could not stand to be with his dad because his dad got mad all the time over little things. The mother worked full-time and tried to manage the home as well. However, she was not at home very much. The mother has a history of major depressive disorder as well as two suicide attempts within the last 3 years. She was hospitalized on each occasion for approximately 2 months. Greg's behavior at home and at school were purported to have been worse than usual during these periods.

At school, Greg was in the fourth grade. His intelligence was within the normal range (full-scale IQ score of 96 on the Wechsler Intelligence Scale for Children—Revised [WISC-R]). Greg's academic performance was behind grade level, and he was in a special class because of his disruptive behavior. His teacher reported that he was overactive and disruptive in class. His parents were told that unless they sought psychological consultation, Greg could not return to the school the next year.

Greg had been in treatment when he was younger. When he was 6 years old, he was seen by his pediatrician for his uncontrollable behavior at home and at school. At that time, he was given stimulant medication to control his overactivity. The mother reported that the medication did not help, and, after about 6 months, she discontinued its use. The parents then brought Greg to an outpatient treatment center for evaluation. They felt that Greg's behavior had become more serious at home and at school and that they did not know where to turn. They talked about giving Greg up or putting him in a special boarding school where more discipline might make him "shape up."

Ann

Ann is a 13-year-old girl who, until recently, lived with her mother and stepfather and her 9-year-old brother. For the last 6 months, she has been living in a youth shelter under the custody of the courts because of repeatedly running away from home. The shelter placement was temporary, pending completion of a court-ordered psychiatric evaluation. Ann was reported by her parents to be oppositional, argumentative, and to lie and steal often. She often stole clothes and jewelry from the homes of relatives and friends, as well as from her parents. In fact, her parents locked their bedroom door and all dresser drawers to protect their valuables. Ann also stole small items from department and discount stores, but this was much less frequent than stealing from other persons.

Running away had been a major problem as well. Over the past 3 years, Ann had run away from home on four occasions. Each time, the police had to be called. Running away was precipitated by being grounded for stealing or smoking cigarettes at home. When Ann was grounded, she was made to remain in her room; however, she usually escaped, even though her room was on the second floor of the home. One time when she escaped and ran away, Ann was gone for 3 nights. The police found her wandering the streets late at night on the other side of town (about 10 miles from her home). Ann would not tell them who she was or where she lived; consequently, several hours elapsed before she was returned home.

During kindergarten, Ann had great difficulty following instructions and making friends. At this time, when Ann was 5, her mother and father were divorced. According to her mother, this period marked the beginning of her antisocial behavior. Ann's school difficulties continued, and teachers complained about her problems in completing school work. Ann's mother moved to a new area, and in the new school, Ann did satisfactory school work and remained at grade level. Teachers said she was smart enough (WISC-R full-scale IQ of 105) to do well, but she had a bad attitude and poor motivation. When she was referred for treatment, she was in the eighth grade and earning Bs, Cs, and Ds in her academic subjects.

Although behavioral problems were evident throughout Ann's history, in the past 3 years they had increased in severity and frequency. At this time, a custody dispute began between her mother and biological father. The dispute began when the father was denied access to the children for one summer because of his excessive drinking. Occasionally, the father would take Ann and her brother to bars where he stayed for several hours and drank. When the custody battle began, tension increased for all family members. As part of the fighting, Ann falsely accused her stepfather of child abuse. This increased efforts of her biological father to obtain custody and also led to a formal investigation of the stepfather. All charges of abuse were eventually dropped. The strain on relations associated with the custody and abuse battle, according to the parents, seemed to precipitate the most recent incident of Ann's running away and was associated with increases in her argumentativeness and unmanageability.

Ann was admitted to an acute care psychiatric hospital for an evaluation. Hospitalization also provided the opportunity to explore the family resources and problems more fully. The goal of the evaluation was to recommend to the court an appropriate placement for Ann, to explore the possibilities of treatment, and to help accelerate resolution of the custody dispute. Eventually, Ann was placed in a foster home and brought to a clinic for individual psychotherapy.

General Comments

These two cases illustrate the type and severity of problems that conduct disorder represents and underscore a few important points. First, in each case, the child engaged in rather severe behaviors. The problems were not merely failing to comply with parental requests, getting into arguments with siblings, engaging in temper tantrums, and failing to complete homework from school. These latter sorts of behaviors were present in each case, but they did not serve as the primary basis for seeking professional attention.

Second, the parents felt that the child was out of control and that their own resources for coping were exhausted. In one case, the school helped to precipitate treatment by making return of the child contingent on seeking professional help. Third, the parents had their own problems and sources of stress, including marital discord, a history of significant psychiatric dysfunction, and unemployment. In one case, three other children were in the home, adding to the difficulties of raising a problem child. Finally, and most obviously, the cases involved several agencies acting on behalf of the child, including the school, the courts, mental health facilities, and a youth service center. Often, conduct disorder youths are in contact with multiple social services.

CLINICAL AND SOCIAL SIGNIFICANCE

The case descriptions illustrate at a personal level some of the problems that conduct disorder represents and the unfortunate circumstances with which it may be associated. Multiplied many times and with broader diversity than two cases can reflect, the personal and social consequences are enormous. The significance of conduct disorder can be underscored by highlighting major characteristics of the problem (see Kazdin, 1993).

Prevalence. The prevalence of conduct disorder, or the proportion of the population with the dysfunction, has been examined in several studies using standardized diagnostic criteria and assessment methods. Estimates of the rate of conduct disorder among children from ages 4 to 18 ranged from approximately 2% to 6% (see Institute of Medicine [IOM], 1989). In the United States, as an example, this means that between 1.3 and 3.8 million children show the disorder.

When specific behaviors that comprise conduct disorder are examined and youths themselves report on their activities, the prevalence rates are extraordinarily high. For example, among youths (ages 13 to 18) more than 50% admit to theft, 35% admit to assault, 45% admit to property destruction, and 60% admit to engaging in more than one type of antisocial behavior, such as aggressive acts, drug abuse, arson, and vandalism (Feldman, Caplinger, & Wodarski, 1983; Williams & Gold, 1972). Even though it is difficult to pinpoint how many children might be identified as having conduct disorder at a particular age, data consistently suggest that the problem is great by most definitions.

Clinic Referrals. Aggressiveness, conduct problems, and antisocial behaviors encompass from one third to one half of all child and adolescent clinic referrals (e.g., Kazdin, Siegel, & Bass, 1990; Robins, 1981). Thus the disorder is one of the most frequent causes of clinical referral.

Stability of the Problem. Among childhood problems, conduct disorder tends to be relatively stable over time (Robins, 1978). The stability departs from many other dysfunctions that remit over the course of development. Thus, when children evince consistent pattern of antisocial behavior, such as aggressive acts toward others, it is unlikely that they will simply "grow out of it."

Prognosis. It follows from the stability of the behavior that the prognosis is likely to be poor. In fact, conduct problems in childhood and adolescence portend later problems in adulthood, including criminal behavior, alcoholism, antisocial personality (i.e., continued conduct disorder), other diagnosable psychiatric disorders, and poor work, marital, and occupational adjustment (Robins, 1966; Wolfgang, Figlio, & Sellin, 1972).

Transmission Across Generations. Antisocial behavior is not only stable over time *within individuals* but also *within families.* Antisocial behavior in childhood predicts similar behaviors in one's offspring. The continuity is evident across multiple generations. Grandchildren are more likely to show antisocial behaviors if their grandparents have a history of these behaviors (Glueck & Glueck, 1968). Also, one of the best predictors of how aggressive a boy will be in childhood is how aggressive his father was when he was about the same age (Huesmann, Eron, Lefkowitz, & Walder, 1984).

Costs to Society. Antisocial behavior is one of the most costly of mental disorders to society (Robins, 1981). The reason is that antisocial youths often remain in continued contact with mental health and criminal justice systems well into adulthood. The costs for psychiatric and psychological treatment, family social work, juvenile adjudication and incarceration, special education programs, and other contacts by social agencies are difficult to estimate. That they are exorbitant is beyond any reasonable doubt.

Absence of Effective Interventions. The significance of conduct disorder is heightened by the absence of clearly effective interventions. Diverse forms of individual and group therapy, behavior therapy, residential treatment, pharmacotherapy, psychosurgery, and a variety of innovative community-based treatments have been applied (for reviews, see Brandt & Zlotnick, 1988; Dumas, 1989; Kazdin, 1985; Pepler & Rubin, 1991). At present, no treatment has been demonstrated to ameliorate conduct disorder and to controvert its poor long-term prognosis. Nevertheless, in the career of the antisocial child and adolescent, several interventions are likely to be tried.

The treatment history of such youths usually begins with early behavioral problems in the school, which may lead to placement in special classes or schools and eventual referral for treatment. At some point later, the individual may be in contact with the judicial system, depending on the specific antisocial behaviors (e.g., stealing, setting fires). Contact with various mental health services may be made, as well as individual referrals for treatment of disruptiveness and unmanageability. Various forms of counseling, psychotherapy, and medication for the child, as well as supportive treatment for the family are likely to be provided. In cases of severe child dysfunction or if families cannot manage the child, or both, referral may be made for inpatient psychiatric hospitalization. Finally, some youths with conduct disorder will be placed outside of the home into foster care, either on a temporary or permanent basis. There is no necessary sequence in which the child traverses these different experiences. However, in the course of treatment and over the course of childhood, adolescence, and adulthood, the individual is likely to be involved in many different services.

Even with only a brief sketch, it is evident that conduct disorder in children and adolescents represents a major social problem. A discussion of the nature and scope of the social problem neglects the personal tragedy that antisocial behavior reflects. There is, of course, the chronic maladjustment and unhappiness of those whose conduct problems are of clinically severe proportions. In addition, there are the many victims of acts of murder, rape, robbery, arson, drunk driving, and spouse or child abuse, which are carried out to a much greater extent by persons with a history of conduct disorder than by other persons. Because of the many victims, antisocial behavior plays a role unlike that of many other psychiatric problems (e.g., depression, psychoses) that dominate research on mental disorders.

DEFINING AND IDENTIFYING ANTISOCIAL BEHAVIORS

Given the case illustrations presented earlier and the types of behaviors that are involved, there should be little difficulty in identifying antisocial acts and the persons who perform them. Actually, not all antisocial behavior comes to the attention of parents, teachers, and professionals who are involved in clinical and legal agencies. Many antisocial behaviors are not attended to or identified as worthy of treatment. There are a number of considerations that are relevant for identifying conduct disorder.

"Normal" Behavior as the Backdrop for Evaluation

Many antisocial behaviors emerge in some form over the course of normal development. Thus the significance and special characteristics of conduct disorder as a clinical problem must be viewed against the backdrop of normal development. Several studies have examined the emergence of antisocial behaviors and their patterns of change over the course of development. The results have indicated surprisingly high prevalence rates for behaviors among samples of normal children and adolescents.

For example, in an early longitudinal study in the field, mothers reported on the problems of their normal children from early childhood through early adolescence (from less than 2 years through 14 years of age) (MacFarlane, Allen, & Honzik, 1954). Among the many noteworthy findings was the relatively high prevalence of specific antisocial behaviors. For example, at age 6, lying was reported as a problem for the majority (53%) of boys. Yet by age 12, the percentage had dropped considerably (to about 10%). For girls, the pattern was more dramatic, with a high rate of lying reported as a problem at age 6 (approximately 48%) and none reported as a problem after age 11. Similarly, a more recent cross-sectional study of children from 4 to 16 years old showed high rates of specific antisocial behaviors (Achenbach, 1991). For example, disobedience at home and destroying other people's things were reported as problems by the parents for approximately 50% and 20% of normal 4- and 5-year-old children. For 16- to 18-year-old adolescents, the rates for these behaviors decreased to approximately 35% and 0%, respectively.

The specific rates of antisocial behavior in these illustrative studies are not to be taken as precise estimates because definitions of antisocial behavior and various measurement methods vary. Also, there are important differences across cultures and countries so that estimates from a given location cannot be generalized. Yet the illustrations convey two points that have some generality—namely, the presence of antisocial behavior is relatively common at different points in normal development. In addition, many of these antisocial behaviors decline over the course of development. Because most children do not show conduct disorder when they mature, early antisocial behavior is not necessarily clinically significant. On the other hand, relatively high rates of antisocial behavior and continued performance rather than a decline of these behaviors represents a clinically significant departure from the normal pattern.

Consideration of antisocial behavior as part of normal development also requires mention of sex differences in these behaviors. Two categories, referred to as externalizing and internalizing behaviors, convey broad patterns of clinical dysfunction. Externalizing (or undercontrolled) behaviors refer to those acts that impinge on others and disrupt the environment. Examples include stealing, fighting, truancy, destructiveness, and lying. Internalizing (or overcontrolled) behaviors refer to characteristics that are more internally focused: anxiety, shyness, withdrawal, hypersensitivity, and physical complaints. As a general statement, boys tend to show higher levels of externalizing types of behaviors over the course of development (e.g., Rutter, Tizard, & Whitmore, 1970). In contrast, girls tend to show greater prevalence of "neurotic" (internalizing) types of symptoms, such as shyness, hypersensitivity, and physical complaints. In general, antisocial behaviors are of the externalizing type and are much more evident in boys and adolescents. Yet sex differences in antisocial behaviors and conduct disorder are more complex than this, as will be elaborated in subsequent chapters.

Even though many antisocial behaviors decline with age for most normal boys and girls, the behaviors are also relatively stable. Stability in this context refers to the correlation of behavior of children assessed on two or more occasions (e.g., a few years apart). The correlation reflects the extent to which children retain their relative standing for the behaviors in their peer group. A high correlation suggests that persons identified as relatively aggressive at one age are also relatively aggressive at a later age. Several longitudinal studies of aggressive behavior with youths ranging in age from 2 to 18 years have found considerable stability of aggressive behavior up to 20, 30, and even 40 years later (see Farrington, 1991; Olweus, 1979). Thus even though rates of aggressive behavior may vary over the course of development, an individual's relative standing among peers appears to be relatively stable.

In general, the identification of serious antisocial behavior requires consideration of developmental norms. Among nonreferred, community samples, antisocial behaviors vary as a function of age and sex. Simply looking for the presence of fighting, stealing, or other behaviors is not enough to decide that a clinical problem exists.

Delineating Conduct Disorder

Many characteristics of the behaviors themselves determine whether clinical levels of severity are evident and hence whether the behavior extends beyond antisocial behavior as part of "normal development." *Frequency and intensity of the behaviors* are central features that determine whether the child is identified as clinically impaired. Obviously, the extent to which a child engages in behaviors such as fighting, stealing, and lying determines whether the behavior warrants attention.

Many antisocial acts are low-frequency, high-intensity behaviors. Their significance stems from the magnitude of their consequences rather than from the actual frequency of the behavior. These are also behaviors that are more severe or extreme relative to variations one might see in the course of normal development. For example, setting fires may be brought to the attention of clinical and legal agencies even if the child has set "only" one or two fires. Similarly, highly dangerous acts of aggression against others, such as attempting to injure a sibling or parent with a weapon or cruel torturing and killing of a pet can serve as a basis for seeking treatment. In such cases, the behaviors are obviously extreme relative to their counterparts in everyday life (e.g., arguments and minor physical fighting between siblings, teasing a pet).

Repetitiveness and chronicity of the acts also help to define clinical levels of antisocial behavior. A single instance of a behavior may not bring the child to the attention of others. Repetition of the act and a protracted history of continuing the behavior over time and across settings can imbue the behaviors with much greater significance. Persistent antisocial behavior reflects the fact that the usual efforts of parents, teachers, and peers and unspecified maturational processes have not had their desired impact.

Multiple antisocial behaviors as a package helps to delineate youths with clinical levels of antisocial behavior. Any specific antisocial act (e.g., fighting) that children show can be viewed as an individual *symptom* or target behavior. Yet antisocial behaviors for many youths come in "packages" or constellations. These packages, referred to as a *syndrome,* emphasize that several different antisocial behaviors are likely to occur together. Conduct disorder as a syndrome includes several core features, such as fighting, stealing, truancy, destroying property, defying or threatening others, and running away. Obviously, any individual child is not likely to show all of the symptoms. The notion that the symptoms are all part of a syndrome merely reflects that they are likely to come in packages.

Impairment in everyday functioning is also critical in separating "normal" antisocial behavior from clinically severe levels. Youths who are functioning poorly in their lives are identified as in need of treatment or some other intervention. Typical signs of impairment in function are (a) repeated problems at school, often leading to detention and occasionally expulsion; (b) unmanageability at home, where the parent cannot manage the child effectively; or (c) dangerous acts that affect others (e.g., peers, siblings). Any of these signs can lead the individual to be identified as having a conduct disorder.

The characteristics highlighted here are considered in combination in the process of identifying clinically severe levels of antisocial behavior. In extreme cases, antisocial children are easily identified by showing all of the characteristics—that is, frequent, severe, chronic, repetitive, and diverse antisocial behaviors. Characteristics of the behaviors are pivotal but not sufficient by themselves to account for clinical referral. Children do not refer themselves for treatment for conduct disorder. Rather adults—typically parents—identify the child as in need of treatment. Parents and other adults do not, of course, share a standard set of definitions, criteria, or thresholds for deciding when this point has been reached. Referral for clinical help depends on a number of factors, such as judgments about the seriousness of the behaviors, judgments about the child or adolescent's functioning, pressures from others (e.g., the schools) to intervene, the availability of other resources (e.g., assistance from relatives in caring for the child), and the parents' actual or perceived inability to manage the child.

Conduct Disorder and Delinquency

Youths who engage in conduct disorder behaviors may be referred to a mental health service and designated with the psychiatric diagnosis of Conduct Disorder or referred to the courts and designated as delinquents. There is an overlap of these designations and of the youths who engage in severe antisocial behavior. Delinquency is based on official contact with the courts. Behaviors that are referred to as delinquent include offenses that are criminal if committed by an adult as well as a variety of behaviors that are illegal because of the age of the youths. The former are referred to as *index offenses* and include such acts as homicide and robbery. The latter are referred to as *status offenses* and involve the use of alcohol, driving a car, staying out late, not attending school, and other behaviors that would not be crimes if the youths were adults. Some of index and status offenses (e.g., arson, truancy) are included in the diagnosis of Conduct Disorder, but others (e.g., selling drugs, prostitution, driving a car while under age) are not.

Conduct Disorder requires a pattern of multiple behaviors that are evident over a period of time (e.g., at least a year). Delinquency differs in the sense that an isolated act or two could lead to arrest. For example, stealing a car would be sufficient to be arrested but not to receive a psychiatric diagnosis of Conduct Disorder. Conduct Disorder youths may or may not engage in behaviors that are defined as delinquent; they may or may not have any contact with the police and courts. Official contact with police is unlikely to take place or to be recorded for young children. Delinquent acts in early and middle childhood are usually dealt with informally rather than officially. On the other hand, Conduct Disorder may be identified and brought to attention early as the child's behavior comes into conflict on a daily basis with parent and teacher expectations.

Characteristics of the psychiatric and legal definitions reflect sources of imprecision that warrant mention. First, the definitions have varied. The criteria for diagnosing Conduct Disorder (e.g., how many symptoms, for what duration) have been revised on several occasions (Robins, 1991). Neither is delinquency a standard, fixed definition because many acts designated as illegal differ from state to state within the United States and, of course, from country to country. Second, both psychiatric and legal definitions are quite broad. To know that someone meets criteria for Conduct Disorder or has been designated as a delinquent does not tell precisely what they have done. There are many ways (e.g., combinations of symptoms, illegal acts) to enter into one of these designations. These definitional issues are not trivial because what we know about conduct disorder has come from the study of youths with one of these designations or who are in settings (clinics, detention centers) where these designations are applied. At this point in our discussion, the critical issue to note is that many of the behaviors of delinquents and conduct disorder youths overlap; the generic term conduct disorder refers to youths who engage in severe antisocial behaviors, whether they are designated by the psychiatric diagnosis of Conduct Disorder or by the legal designation of delinquency, or whether they are not referred to services at all.

CONDUCT DISORDER YOUTHS AND THEIR FAMILIES

Antisocial behaviors that emerge over the course of normal development are likely to be isolated, short-lived, and relatively mild. When the behaviors are extreme, do not remit over the course of development, affect the child's daily functioning, and have important implications for others (e.g., parents, teachers, peers), children are often brought to clinical attention. The antisocial behaviors then, of course, are viewed as significant departures from normal behavior and these children are often identified through mental health agencies or the courts.

Correlates and Associated Features

The behaviors that define or are central to conduct disorder (e.g., fighting, stealing, truancy, lying, setting fires, and others) are not the only characteristics of such youths. Other characteristics also affect diverse facets of functioning. These are referred to as correlates or associated features rather than as defining characteristics. Among alternative symptoms associated with conduct disorder, those related to *hyperactivity* have been the most frequently identified. These symptoms include excesses of motor activity, restlessness, impulsiveness, inattentiveness, and overactivity in general. In fact, the co-occurrence of hyperactivity and conduct disorder has made their diagnostic delineation and assessment a topic of considerable research. Several other behaviors have been identified as problematic among antisocial youths, such as boisterousness, showing off, and blaming others. Many of these appear to be relatively mild forms of obstreperous behavior in comparison to aggression, theft, vandalism, or other acts that invoke damage to persons or property.

Children and adolescents with conduct disorder behaviors are also likely to show *academic deficiencies,* as reflected in achievement levels, grades, and specific skill areas, particularly reading (e.g., Ledingham & Schwartzman, 1984; Sturge, 1982). Such children are often seen by their teachers as uninterested in school, unenthusiastic toward academic pursuits, and careless in their work. As would be expected from these characteristics, conduct disorder children are more likely to be left behind in grades, to show lower achievement levels, and to end their schooling sooner than peers matched in age, socioeconomic status, and other demographic variables (e.g., Bachman, Johnston, & O'Malley, 1978; Glueck & Glueck, 1968).

Poor interpersonal relations are likely to correlate with antisocial behavior. Children high in aggressiveness or other antisocial behaviors are often rejected by their peers and show poor social skills (e.g., Behar & Stewart, 1982; Carlson, Lahey, & Neeper, 1984). Such youths have been found to be socially ineffective in their interactions with an array of adults (e.g., parents, teachers, community members) and engage in behaviors that promote deleterious interpersonal consequences for themselves.

The correlates of antisocial behavior involve not only overt behaviors but also a variety of *cognitive and attributional processes* (e.g., Crick & Dodge, 1994; Shirk, 1988). Antisocial youths have been found to be deficient in cognitive problem-solving skills that underlie social interaction. For example, such youths are more likely than their peers to interpret gestures of others as hostile and are less able to identify solutions to interpersonal problem situations and to take the perspective of others.

These symptoms, correlated behaviors, and areas of impairment refer to *concurrent* problems that are likely to be evident in the behavior of clinically impaired children. A number of characteristics continue to emerge over time, as discussed in subsequent chapters.

Parent and Family Characteristics

Several characteristics of the parents and families of conduct disorder youths are relevant to conceptualization of the dysfunction as well as to assessment and intervention (see Kazdin, 1993). Among the salient characteristics are parent psychopathology and maladjustment. Parents have higher rates of clinical dysfunction. Criminal behavior and alcoholism, particularly of the father, are two parental characteristics often associated with conduct disorder. Certain disciplinary practices and attitudes are also associated with conduct disorder. Parents are likely to show especially harsh, lax, erratic, or inconsistent discipline practices. Dysfunctional family relations are also evident as reflected in less acceptance of their children; less warmth, affection, and emotional support; and less attachment than found among parents of non-referred youths. At the level of family relations, less supportive and more defensive communications between family members, less participation in activities as a family, and more clear dominance of one family member are also evident. In addition, unhappy marital relations, interpersonal conflict, and aggression characterize the parental relations of antisocial children.

Contextual Conditions

A variety of circumstances in which youths live are relevant both to conceptualization of dysfunction and interventions. Examples of relevant factors include large family size, overcrowding, poor housing, poor parental supervision, high crime neighborhoods, and disadvantaged school settings. Many of the untoward conditions in which families live place stress on the parent or diminish the threshold for coping with everyday stressors. The net effect can be evident in parent-child interaction in which parents inadvertently engage in patterns that sustain or accelerate antisocial and aggressive interactions. Also, contextual factors (e.g., poor living conditions) bring with them other influences (e.g., deviant and aggressive peer groups, poor supervision of the child) that can have their own influences on the child. For example, some young children we have seen in our clinic carry weapons (e.g., knives and guns) just because carrying a weapon is considered necessary so they will not be bullied by others. Accepting this interpretation for the moment, it is still quite problematic because the step from carrying to using a weapon may not be very great.

THREE VIGNETTES

Child, parent, family, and contextual characteristics are highlighted merely to place the disorder in a broader perspective. At the same time, the discussion does not convey the flavor of the cases that come to treatment. Consider three brief vignettes that better convey the contexts and situations in which conduct disorder is embedded. The vignettes are drawn from cases referred to an outpatient clinic devoted to the treatment of children (ages 3 to 13) seen for conduct disorder.

Vignette 1: Family Values

In this case, the mother was referred to our clinic by her son's school because of his high rate of fighting and repeated school suspensions. The mother telephoned our clinic and scheduled an appointment for an intake evaluation. She did not show up, nor did she call to cancel or reschedule the appointment. There was no answer at her residence and no further contact was made with her at this time. About 4 months later, she called again, scheduled another appointment, and a few days later came for our initial evaluation. She and her son (10 years old) completed the intake evaluation, which included several measures. As part of the conversation during the day of assessment, the clinician asked about the prior call about 4 months earlier and noted how good it was that she came in. The mother apologized for not showing up for the prior appointment. She stated that she was unable to come in because she "broke a family rule." Of course, the clinician asked what that reason was. The mother reported that she and her husband, and for that matter a number of their relatives, often shoot each other (with guns). However, there is one family rule: "You *never* shoot someone in public." The mother said she broke this rule; some neighbors saw her shoot her husband, and she spent 3 months in prison. Now that she is out of prison, she said, she is ready for her son to begin treatment.

**Vignette 2: Multiple Sources
of Dysfunction and Stress**

In another one of our cases, the mother was a single parent with two young boys (ages 2 and 4). She sought treatment because her older son was engaging in relatively severe and uncontrollable aggressive behaviors, including hitting, kicking, and biting the younger sibling. The mother was currently diagnosed as clinically depressed and was on medication for depression. She had a prior suicide attempt and, at the time of intake, was at risk for suicide, based on her reporting of suicidal ideation. Her boyfriend is the father of the two children. He lives nearby and calls her a couple times a week. In these calls, he demands that she come over so he can see the children. During these visits, he engages her in what she referred to as "forced sex" (i.e., rape), and he demands that the two children remain with them and watch. In principle, the mother could have refused the visits. However, the boyfriend threatened that if she did not comply, he would stop paying child support, take the children away in a custody battle, kill himself, or come over to the house and kill her and the two children. These threats of violence were to be taken seriously as the boyfriend had a prior arrest record for assault and brandished a gun. He fueled the mother's fears regarding loss of the children by saying that he would take the children in a custody battle in the courts. The mother, who was in psychotherapy for depression and suicidal ideation, said that she could end it all by just driving the children and herself over a cliff. Our involvement in the case was for the treatment of the older child and his aggressive behavior.

Vignette 3: Violence in the Home

Parent and family issues affect referral to treatment and diagnosis as well. One case was a 12-year-old boy, named Steve, referred for treatment because he stabbed his father and stole a car. He had a history of antisocial behavior, primarily lying, fighting at school, and theft, and he was in constant trouble with school personnel and police. Further details emerged about the reason for referral during a diagnostic interview with the child. During the interview, Steve readily admitted that he stabbed his father in the leg. But his story included some interesting details that had not come up previously. He and his two brothers were in their parents' bedroom while the mother was being raped by the father. She was screaming for help and panicked. Steve went and got a knife from the kitchen; his brothers tried to restrain him but could do so only partially. Steve stabbed his father in the calf, deeply and with a long cut. After the stabbing, Steve felt he was going to get beaten, because his father had a long history of physically abusing the boys. He fled to his grandfather's house, took the keys of the car without permission or awareness, drove off, and crashed the car in a field. The child was brought to us by the police. By all accounts, Steve stabbed his father. And indeed he stole a car.

General Comments

These vignettes are not extreme examples in the day-to-day business of clinical care of conduct disorder children and their families, as would be readily acknowledged by others involved in clinical practice. The vignettes underscore a central point, namely that quite often the child's dysfunction is embedded in a larger context that cannot be neglected in conceptual views about the development, maintenance, and course of conduct disorder, nor in the actual delivery of treatment.

Conduct disorder can be conceived as a dysfunction of children and adolescents. The accumulated evidence regarding the symptom constellation, risk factors, and course over childhood, adolescence, and adulthood attests to the heuristic value of focusing on individual children. At the same time, there is a child-parent-family-context *gestalt* that includes multiple and reciprocal influences that affect each participant (i.e., child and parent) and the systems in which they operate (i.e., family, school). The gestalt poses challenges for developing models of dysfunction as well as for identifying effective treatments.

SUMMARY AND OVERVIEW
OF REMAINING CHAPTERS

Conduct disorder represents a major clinical and social problem. The behaviors, particularly aggression, are relatively frequent and account for the major portion of clinical referrals. Antisocial behaviors wax and wane over the course of normal development. When the behaviors are frequent, intense, and chronic, they raise a special problem. Children with clinically severe antisocial behaviors are likely to continue these behaviors as adolescents and adults. Moreover, the problems do not end in adulthood but continue through the offspring, so the cycle is sustained.

The personal or nonmonetary costs are monumental as well. Each individual story represents a personal tragedy. Sympathy for the conduct disorder child or adolescent is easily evoked by detailing the personal situations and influences from which many such youths emerge. The sympathy is often lost when turning to the victims of antisocial acts, who may have had chance contact with antisocial youths and were beaten, robbed, burned, or victimized in some other way. The salience of conduct disorder is augmented even further by the absence of clearly effective treatments. Thus the clinical and social problems of conduct disorder thrive; the solutions in terms of understanding the dysfunctions and identifying steps to ameliorate them have a long germination period that has only just begun.

In subsequent chapters, the characteristics of conduct disorder will be elaborated. In Chapter 2, I will consider the diagnosis and assessment of conduct disorder. Current diagnostic criteria, age and sex variations of conduct problem behaviors, alternative ways of identifying patterns or subtypes of these behaviors, and strategies to measure conduct disorder are examined. In Chapter 3, the onset and course of conduct disorder are considered. This chapter examines the risk and protective factors related to the onset of conduct disorder and considers how the factors may operate over the course of development.

In Chapters 4 and 5, treatment and prevention are examined. The range of interventions that has been applied to antisocial youths or those who are at risk for conduct disorder is vast. Among the many innovative programs, only a few have been carefully evaluated and show promise at this point. The different programs, current status of research, and the obstacles and prospects for identifying effective interventions are also presented in Chapters 4 and 5.

In Chapter 6, approaches to the conceptualization, diagnosis, and treatment of conduct disorder are evaluated. Current work raises questions about the limitations of the approaches currently dominating the field. In this, the final chapter, new models are suggested that are designed to accelerate the rate of progress in ameliorating conduct disorder in children and adolescents.

NOTES

1. The terms *normal* and *normal development* warrant comment. In the context of emotional and behavioral problems, the notion of normal is often discussed as if it were a qualitative state and distinguishable from *abnormal*. Youths seen in treatment settings often are referred to as a clinical sample and distinguished from normal children of the same age. Yet research shows that many youths (17% to 22%) functioning well in everyday life nonetheless show significant levels of clinical symptoms and impairment (IOM, 1989; Zill & Schoenborn, 1990). Thus, with a sample referred to as normal, a significant degree of impairment may be evident. Whether a youth comes   treatment is not necessarily due to a difference between normal and abnormal states, out involves many other factors (e.g., availability of services, types of symptoms that a youth shows, stress on the parents). In the present text, normal will be used to refer to normative in the sense of what most individuals do at that age and level of development.

2. The term *conduct disorder* here is used generically to delineate clinically severe levels of dysfunction. The term *Conduct Disorder* also refers to a specific constellation of behaviors in psychiatric diagnosis. The generic and specific uses of these terms overlap. The proper noun will be used when the specific diagnostic category is delineated, as elaborated in the next chapter.

2

DIAGNOSIS AND ASSESSMENT

Information about how conduct disorder comes about, what can be done in the way of treatment, and the likely long-term course of the disorder all depend on identifying cases, that is, individuals who show the dysfunction. Individuals can vary widely in severity and type of dysfunction so that the presence or absence of conduct disorder in an either-or fashion is not always clear. Yet for scientific advances, it is essential to specify the criteria to delineate clinical dysfunction and to identify various symptom patterns. These objectives entail interrelated lines of work on the diagnosis and assessment of conduct disorder. The present chapter considers conduct disorder as formal psychiatric diagnosis and subtypes of conduct disorder. In addition, assessment methods are discussed and illustrated because measurement is central to research designed to understand, treat, and prevent conduct disorder.

DIAGNOSIS OF CONDUCT DISORDER

Diagnostic Criteria

The purpose of developing diagnostic criteria is to understand the patterns of functioning, how they emerge, their course, and how they can be treated and prevented. To achieve these goals, one wishes to develop ways of defining the pattern so it can be studied. At the same time as the pattern is studied, the ways of defining the pattern may be shown to be inadequate, in need of revision, or, at worst, misguided. The dilemma is apparent in the very task, namely, to define a pattern of dysfunction before all or indeed very much information is available. Diagnosis of emotional and behavioral problems is much more difficult than diagnosis of many physical problems, although physical problems raise perplexing dilemmas as well. But for most emotional and behavioral problems, there is no objective test (e.g., series of blood tests for mononucleosis) or sequence of events (e.g., animal bite, foaming at the mouth of the patient, and death in the case of rabies) that reveals the fairly certain presence of a disorder.

The benefits of diagnosis are evident from experience and knowledge from medical disorders in everyday life. We know, for example, for many symptoms with which we have common experience (e.g., sore throat, high fever, aches and pains) that a diagnosis can have important implications for treatment (e.g., antibiotics). Beyond that, understanding a disorder and its origin can lead to prevention (e.g., not smoking to diminish chances of lung cancer).

Diagnosis of emotional and behavioral problems is designed to capture these and many other benefits, although there are spirited discussions whether diagnosis of problems of everyday life is analogous to medical disease. Currently, diagnosis of emotional and behavioral disorders is dominated by a categorical approach.[1] Categorical diagnosis refers to the identification of discrete constellations of behaviors or syndromes. Whether a disorder is present depends on several conditions, including whether various symptoms are present, whether enough symptoms are present to meet criteria for the disorder, whether the symptoms have been evident long enough over time, and whether they interfere with or impair functioning in everyday life. These conditions convey the complex tasks of diagnosis. The diagnosis is categorical because the person does or does not meet criteria for the disorder. However, decisions along the way are often a matter of degree. Thus the individual may have the characteristic (e.g., sadness for depression) but a decision needs to be made whether it is severe enough to be counted as a symptom (e.g., does it impair functioning) and then, if it has been present enough to be counted as a symptom. There are measures to help make these decisions.

Several different diagnostic systems have been developed. The two dominant systems are the *Diagnostic and Statistical Manual of Mental Disorders* (*DSM*; American Psychiatric Association [APA], 1994) and the *International Classification of Diseases* (*ICD*; World Health Organization [WHO], 1992). These systems are very similar in their focus and in many of the definitions of specific disorders. There are differences that emerge from how they were developed and in how they are used. The *Diagnostic and Statistical Manual*, or *DSM* as it is called, is the most commonly used diagnostic system throughout the world

TABLE 2.1 Symptoms Included in the Diagnosis of Conduct Disorder

---

Aggression to people and animals
1. often bullies, threatens, or intimidates others
2. often initiates physical fights
3. has used a weapon that can cause serious physical harm to others
   (e.g., a bat, brick, broken bottle, knife, gun)
4. has been physically cruel to people
5. has been physically cruel to animals
6. has stolen while confronting a victim
   (e.g., mugging, purse snatching, extortion, armed robbery)
7. has forced someone into sexual activity

Destruction of property
8. has deliberately engaged in setting fires with the intention of causing serious damage
9. has deliberately destroyed others' property (other than by setting fires)

Deceitfulness or theft
10. has broken into someone else's house, building, or car
11. often lies to obtain goods or favors or to avoid obligations (i.e., "cons" others)
12. has stolen items of nontrivial value without confronting a victim
    (e.g., shoplifting, but without breaking and entering; forgery)

Serious violations of rules
13. often stays out at night despite parental prohibitions, beginning before age 13
14. has run away from home overnight at least twice while living in parental or parental
    surrogate home (or once without returning for a lengthy period)
15. is often truant from school, beginning before age 13

NOTE: The symptom list here is based on the fourth edition of the *Diagnostic and Statistical Manual of Mental Disorders* (*DSM-IV*, APA, 1994). The number of symptoms required to meet criteria for the diagnosis of Conduct Disorder is at least 3 symptoms that have occurred within the past 12 months, at least 1 of which has been in the last 6 months.

(Maser, Kaelber, & Weise, 1991). The *DSM* has been revised on several occasions (1968, 1980, 1987, 1994) to reflect advances in our understanding of disorders as well as to reflect changes in society in thinking about deviance and what ought to be called mental illness. The most recent version is the fourth edition (*DSM-IV*).

The major diagnostic category within *DSM-IV* for coding antisocial behavior in children and adolescents is Conduct Disorder.[2] The essential feature is a pattern of behavior in which the child has ignored the rights of others or has violated age-appropriate norms and roles. In order for the diagnosis to be made, a specific set of problematic behaviors must be present and must have a duration of several months. Table 2.1 illustrates the type of symptoms that are included. In the *DSM-IV*, a

TABLE 2.2 Diagnostic Categories Other Than Conduct Disorder That
Include Antisocial Behaviors

Disorder or Condition and Key Characteristics

Oppositional Defiant Disorder: A pattern of negativistic, defiant, disobedient, and hostile
behavior toward authority figures as evident in such behaviors as temper tantrums, argumentativeness, refusing to comply with requests, and deliberately annoying others. Usually
aggression toward others, destruction of property, and more severe behaviors of Conduct
Disorder are not evident. The onset is usually before the age of 8.

Adjustment Disorder With Disturbance of Conduct: Clinically significant emotional and
behavioral symptoms that occur in response to an identifiable stressor (e.g., divorce, loss of a
relative). The symptoms develop within 3 months of the onset of that stressor and appear to
be a direct reaction to that event. This diagnosis is reserved for those situations in which the
symptoms include Conduct Disorder symptoms such as fighting, vandalism, and truancy.

Antisocial Personality Disorder: A pervasive pattern of disregard for, and violation of, the
rights of others including such acts as assault, destroying property, harassing others, stealing,
illegal activity whether or not detected, driving while intoxicated, and related activities. The
diagnosis includes a pattern of continuous antisocial behavior. For this diagnosis, the individual must be at least 18 years old and have had a history of symptoms of Conduct Disorder
before the age of 15.

Other Conditions That May Be a Focus of Clinical Attention: Isolated antisocial acts in
childhood or adolescence rather than a pattern of antisocial behavior that suggests a longer
term mental disorder. This category is reserved for those isolated acts when other diagnostic
criteria cannot be invoked.

---

diagnosis of Conduct Disorder is provided if (a) the individual shows
at least three symptoms of those listed, (b) the symptoms were evident
within the past 12 months, and (c) at least one of the symptoms was
evident in the past 6 months.

Characteristics of Conduct Disorder may be evident in other diagnostic categories. Table 2.2 lists a number of diagnoses in which similar
behaviors may also be evident. For each of these diagnoses, a critical
feature such as age of onset or severity and duration of the behavior
differs from that of Conduct Disorder. Oppositional Defiant Disorder is
especially worth highlighting because the typical behaviors included
in this diagnosis are likely to be evident in Conduct Disorder. However, children with a diagnosis of Oppositional Defiant Disorder do not
show the major rule violations and serious antisocial acts of Conduct
Disorder.

**Ambiguities and Sources
of Controversy Briefly Noted**

The *DSM* provides explicit criteria and is designed to permit the study of various disorders so that progress can be made both in understanding and in defining the disorders themselves. This task is important to note because of its difficulty. There is no single completely defensible set of defining criteria that can be said to "really" define conduct disorder. Over many revisions of the *DSM*, the criteria have changed (Robins, 1991). In early versions, Conduct Disorder was not included as a disorder; in later revisions, the criteria have changed and subtypes have changed. There is agreement in the field that Conduct Disorder (i.e., clinically severe levels of antisocial behavior) is a problem identifiable in youths. There are debates in relation to contemporary diagnosis regarding the criteria of how to identify such youths.

Some of the more salient issues are important to note in passing because they convey challenges for the field. First, the criteria for reaching a diagnosis of Conduct Disorder can be challenged (e.g., why three symptoms are the minimum required to meet the diagnosis instead of four or five; why a 12-month period is required for the symptoms to be present instead of a longer or shorter period). These questions are not a matter of quibbling over trivia because they determine who is included in research on Conduct Disorder and hence what we consider to be the characteristics of such youths.

Second, the overlap of disorders related to Conduct Disorder has raised fundamental questions about how to divide emotional and behavioral problems. For example, Conduct Disorder and Oppositional Defiant Disorder often occur together. Among clinically referred youths who meet criteria for Conduct Disorder, 84% to 96% also meet criteria for Oppositional Defiant Disorder (Hinshaw, Lahey, & Hart, 1993). Similarly, in studies of community and clinic samples, a large percentage of youths diagnosed with Conduct Disorder or Attention-Deficit/Hyperactivity Disorder also meet criteria for the other disorder (e.g., Fergusson, Horwood, & Lloyd, 1991; Offord, Boyle, & Racine, 1991). The overlap raises questions about the categories themselves and about what is the most meaningful and useful way to delineate disruptive behaviors.

Third, the symptoms are delineated in a fixed way so that they are applied equally across the full period of childhood and adolescence. Yet perhaps symptoms required to meet the diagnosis should vary with age. It is unlikely that a 4-year-old would steal or confront a victim or force sex on someone. Does this mean that Conduct Disorder does not emerge before the age of 4 years or that the criteria for a 4-year-old ought to be different? This chapter will consider variations of conduct problems as a function of sex and age and hence it will elaborate this concern.

DEVELOPMENTAL VARIATIONS IN CONDUCT DISORDER

Sex Differences

The prevalence rate of conduct disorder (2% to 6% among community samples of youths) was mentioned in the previous chapter. One of the most frequent findings is that boys show higher rates of conduct disorder than girls. In general, conduct disorder is 3 to 4 times more common in boys than girls (see Zoccolillo, 1993). Yet the precise sex ratio is difficult to specify because of varying criteria, measures of conduct disorder, and ages at which point youths are measured. Sex differences are found in clinic and community samples and across different types of measures, such as parent and youth reports of antisocial behavior.

The differences between sexes is subject to many different interpretations, including bias in the way in which conduct disorder is defined. Consider briefly some of the issues. To begin, in the course of normal development, boys and girls often differ in a variety of behaviors—for example, engaging in rough and tumble play, bullying others, not complying with requests, and fighting (e.g., Achenbach, 1991; Maccoby, 1986). The higher base rates for these and other behaviors for boys means that more deviant instances need to be evident to stand out and to be clinically important. These behaviors are likely to have low rates in girls, both with community and clinically referred samples. Perhaps when a few instances of antisocial behaviors are evident in girls, they are more clinically significant. For example, consider fighting as a case in point. Getting into one or two fights for a boy and for a girl may have a somewhat different meaning in light of cultural expectations and different base rates. A girl getting into one or two fights is much more extreme (in comparison to her female peers) than the "same" actions of a boy. This could be discussed as a cultural interpretive bias, different expectations, and so on. The fact is the base rates are different for these behaviors, and the different base rates imbue different significances to the behaviors when they emerge. In general, in the diagnosis of Conduct Disorder, the symptoms that are listed favor boys because they focus on those confrontive and violent actions that are more likely in boys (Zoccolillo, 1993).

Evidence increasingly points to sex differences in many facets of conduct disorder. The factors that predict the onset of conduct disorder differ for boys and girls. When conduct disorder emerges, development tends to differ as well; conduct disorder is more likely to emerge in childhood for boys and in adolescence for girls. Also, the short- and long-term effects appear to differ. Conduct disorder boys are more likely to engage in criminal behavior when they become adolescents than are conduct disorder girls, and the boys are more likely to be arrested as a result. As they become adults, males with a history of conduct disorder are more likely to continue antisocial behavior, whereas girls with a history of conduct disorder are more likely to shift into depression and anxiety as adults (Robins & Rutter, 1990). In subsequent discussions, sex differences will be elaborated further to convey quite different patterns of conduct disorder.

Age Variations

Conduct Disorder is defined as a disorder that arises in childhood. From a developmental perspective, it is useful to note that a pattern of aggressive, antisocial, and disruptive behavior can be evident over the life span. The difficulty in recognizing the patterns has to do with the fact that the precise ways in which these behaviors may be evident change over development. For example, stealing from others, robbing a store, and forcing sexual activity are easily seen in youths 7 to 12 years old, but not in infants. What kind of behaviors ought one to look for at a young age, particularly at a very young age? (A sibling of a child seen at our outpatient clinic was only 9 months old when he was expelled from day care for punching other children.)

Age variations reveal interesting patterns. In general, rates of conduct disorder tend to be higher for adolescents (approximately 7% for 12- to 16-year-olds) than for children (approximately 4% for 4- to 11-year-olds) (Offord et al., 1991). Adolescent girls and youths who engage in nonaggressive forms of antisocial behavior (e.g., truancy, running away) seem to be responsible for this increase.

Sex differences are apparent in the age of onset of dysfunction. Robins (1966) found that the median age of onset of dysfunction for children referred for antisocial behavior was in the 8- to 10-year-old age range. Most boys (57%) had an onset before the age of 10 (median = 7 years old). For girls, onset of antisocial behavior was concentrated in the 14- to 16-year-old age range (median = 13 years old). Characteristic symptom patterns were different as well. Theft and aggression were more likely to serve as a basis of referral among antisocial boys. For girls, antisocial behavior was much more likely to include sexual misbehavior.

Recent research has suggested that the age of onset of conduct disorder may be significant in relation to clinical course (Hinshaw et al., 1993). Symptoms emerging in childhood are likely to be types of aggression whereas symptoms emerging in adolescence are more likely to relate to stealing. The symptoms emerging in childhood are associated with a relatively poor prognosis, whereas the symptoms emerging in adolescence tend to have a better prognosis. These differences are elaborated in the following discussion of subtypes of conduct disorder.

SUBTYPES OF CONDUCT DISORDER

Children with the Conduct Disorder diagnosis can vary widely in terms of the specific symptoms as well as the associated features (e.g., academic deficiencies, parent dysfunction). A central question for the field is whether there are meaningful ways to divide the class into subgroups. Several lines of work have focused on identifying how conduct disorder unfolds, its varied manifestations, and its paths. From the standpoint of diagnosis, the effort has been to identify subtypes of youths whose features, onset, course, response to treatment, and so on vary systematically. Salient subtypes are highlighted here.

Aggressive and Delinquent Types

One of the better studied and demonstrated means of subtyping conduct disorder has been the delineation of aggressive and delinquent types. These different types have emerged from efforts to identify patterns of symptoms that correlate with each other and form a constellation of symptoms. Statistical techniques (e.g., factor analyses) can be used to identify groups of symptoms (e.g., items from the measures) that go together. From these groups of symptoms, one can then identify (e.g., via cluster analysis) whether there are patterns within individuals (see Achenbach, 1993a). Aggressive and delinquent patterns of symptoms have consistently emerged from such analyses. *Aggressive* conduct disorder youths are likely to engage in fighting, property destruction, cruelty to other people or to animals; *delinquent* youths are likely to engage in theft, running away, lying, setting fires, and truancy from school. In the past, aggressive and delinquent types have been considered along with another dimension—namely, whether youths engage in conduct problem behavior in a group or alone. However, group versus solitary behavior is not as strongly supported as a way of subtyping conduct disorder (Achenbach, 1993b).

Aggressive versus delinquent subtypes have been well supported by research. Of the two subtypes, the stronger evidence pertains to the aggressive subtype. Also, the aggressive subtype appears to be more stable over the course of development (Achenbach, 1993b). Worth noting is that the two types are not mutually exclusive. Even though many youths might fall into one or the other type, some will have both.

Aggressors and Stealers

Some other efforts to develop subtypes overlap with aggressive and delinquent subtypes but have shades of difference worth noting. One such scheme focuses on salient or key symptoms, distinguishing youngsters whose primary symptom is aggression (*aggressors*) from those whose primary symptom is stealing (*stealers*) (Patterson, 1982). Aggressors have a history of fighting and engaging in assaultive behavior; stealers have a history of repeated theft and contacts with the courts. Although these characteristics often go together, subpopulations of "pure" aggressors or stealers can be readily identified. Aggressive children have been found to engage in significantly more aversive and coercive behaviors in their interactions in the home and are less compliant with parents' requests than are children who steal (Patterson, 1982). Also, parents of stealers show greater emotional distance in relation to their children (e.g., lack of responding, less disapproval, fewer commands) than do parents of aggressors. Other studies have shown that the prognosis of antisocial children may vary as a function of whether they have been identified as aggressors or stealers. For example, subsequent contact with the courts several years later is significantly more likely for children previously identified as stealers than aggressors (Moore,

Chamberlain, & Mukai, 1979). Many children may be both aggressors and stealers, although this group has been less well studied.

Overt and Covert Antisocial Behavior

The focus on aggressors and stealers has been expanded to consider a broader, bipolar dimension of overt and covert behavior (Loeber, Lahey, & Thomas, 1991). *Overt behaviors* consist of those antisocial acts that are confrontive (such as fighting, arguing, and temper tantrums). *Covert behaviors,* on the other hand, consist of concealed acts (such as stealing, truancy, lying, substance abuse, and setting fires). Aggressors and stealers can be represented by the notions of overt and covert behavior, although this approach draws attention to a slightly different aspect of the youths.

Support for this domain emerged from an analysis of a large number of studies of antisocial behavior of school-age children (Loeber & Schmaling, 1985). Statistical analyses of the grouping of antisocial behaviors across studies supported the dimension of overt and covert behavior. A cluster of overt behaviors and a cluster of covert behaviors emerged. Thus the presence of one behavior in the cluster means that other behaviors of that cluster are likely to be present as well. Some behaviors such as disobedience and sassiness tended to be present with both clusters of antisocial behavior.

Support for the distinction between overt and covert behavior draws on the evidence for aggressors and stealers mentioned previously. Also, other studies have suggested that overt and covert behavior problems are associated with varied child and family characteristics. For example, children higher in overt conduct problems are more irritable, negative, and resentful in their reactions to hostile situations, and they experience more family conflict (Kazdin, 1992a). Children higher in covert antisocial behavior are less social, more anxious, view others more suspiciously, and come from homes lower in family cohesion.

Given the complexity and diversity of antisocial behaviors, one would expect that some children are likely to perform both overt and covert behaviors (i.e., reflect a "mixed" set of behaviors). Mixed types of children are distinguished from "purer" types by more severe family dysfunction and poorer long-term prognoses (e.g., manifested in subsequent contacts with police and in careers of antisocial behavior). Thus children whose antisocial behaviors are diverse or mixed (i.e., overt and covert) may be at high risk for long-term dysfunction (Robins, 1978).

Recent data have suggested that mixed types include multiple combinations of overt and covert behavior alone and in combination with other characteristics of dysfunction such as conflict with authority (Loeber et al., 1993).

Child and Adolescent Onset

Recently, increased attention has focused on the period of onset for conduct disorder (see Hinshaw et al., 1993; Moffitt, 1993a; Patterson, DeBaryshe, & Ramsey, 1989). (The impact of this particular method of subtyping has led to its adoption within the *DSM* as different patterns of antisocial behavior.) Two types of conduct disorder have been identified based on whether the symptoms emerge in childhood or adolescence. *Child-onset conduct disorder* consists of youths whose dysfunction is evident early in childhood, beginning with Oppositional Defiant Disorder or possibly Attention-Deficit/Hyperactivity Disorder. The symptoms progress to those of conduct disorder, even though many of the youths retain the symptoms from these other diagnoses. Child-onset conduct disorder is the more severe form of conduct disorder. Youths with this form of the disorder are more likely to engage in aggressive and criminal behaviors, and they are likely to continue their dysfunction into adulthood.

Adolescent-onset conduct disorder is more common than the child-onset type. During adolescence, many youths engage in criminal behavior. For many of these youths, such acts are isolated; for others, the pattern meets criteria for Conduct Disorder. Youngsters with both child- and adolescent-onset conduct disorder engage in illegal behavior during adolescence. However, those with child onset are more likely to engage in aggressive acts and are more likely to be boys. The adolescent-onset type is more equally distributed among girls and boys. Stated another way, conduct disorder among girls is more likely to have an onset in adolescence. Peers are considered to play a central role in the emergence and onset of adolescent conduct disorder.

Evidence for the increased incidence of nonaggressive Conduct Disorder at about the age of 15 with no corresponding increase in aggressive Conduct Disorder has served as support for the notion that a group can be identified with adolescent onset (McGee, Feehan, Williams, & Anderson, 1992; Patterson, 1992). Differences in neuropsychological, sympathetic, and neuroendocrine functions have been proposed to relate to the different subtypes (see Hinshaw et al., 1993; Moffitt, 1993a).

Evidence suggests that parent management practices may contribute to child onset by inadvertently promoting aversive behavior in the child. Negative reinforcement of deviant behavior; inattention to positive, prosocial behavior; and coercive interactions between parent and child lead to escalation of aggressive child behavior. This in turn leads to stable patterns of child aggression that has other consequences (e.g., poor peer relations, association with deviant peers, school failure) (Patterson, Capaldi, & Bank, 1991).

Other Variations

Other ways of subtyping conduct disorder children have been proposed. One proposal focuses on aggressive behavior and suggests that there are two types—namely, aggression that is *reactive* (in response to others) versus aggression that is *proactive* (as an initial way of goal attainment) (Dodge, 1991). Proactively aggressive children use aggression to obtain goals by dominating and coercing others. The reactively aggressive child is easily provoked, in part by perceiving others as having hostile intentions, and responds aggressively. Support for these types has come from research showing that proactively and reactively aggressive youths (or youths with both types) are perceived differently by peers and teachers and differ in their ability to solve interpersonal problems (e.g., Day, Bream, & Pal, 1992).

Another proposal delineates compound disorders. For example, as already noted, Conduct Disorder is often present with Attention-Deficit/Hyperactivity Disorder. Conduct Disorder, in combination with Attention-Deficit/Hyperactivity Disorder, has distinct characteristics when compared to pure cases of either one of the disorders. This suggests that the combination may constitute a separate type of dysfunction (Szatmari, Boyle, & Offord, 1989). This combination is only one such combination that may be identifiable insofar as Conduct Disorder can combine with many other conditions (Zoccolillo, 1992). Developing subtypes of Conduct Disorder on the basis of the comorbid (coexisting) conditions is one approach to identifying meaningful types and is evident in the *International Classification of Diseases* (WHO, 1992). Examining combined sets of disorders may be useful in its own right, but this is different from efforts to identify patterns within the class of conduct disorder symptoms.

Efforts to identify various subtypes are very important to progress. The individual efforts serve as the basis for developing empirical tests of other characteristics of the disorder (e.g., history, long-term course). The diversity of proposed subtypes could be viewed as a indicating that conceptual chaos prevails, that little is known, or that several different testable models have been developed to serve as a basis for further advances. A noteworthy consistency is the importance of distinguishing an aggressive type (e.g., fighting) from a delinquent type (e.g., criminal behavior, running away, lying). The characteristics, prognoses, and developmental sequence of these different subtypes of antisocial behaviors may be important.

The search for specific subtypes of antisocial behavior is not the only way that conduct disorder has been considered. Research has supported a broader level of evaluating antisocial behavior. Problem behaviors often go together so that individuals with one (e.g., delinquent acts) are likely to show other behaviors (e.g., early sexual activity, drug abuse) as well (Elliott, Huizinga, & Menard, 1988; Jessor, Donovan, & Costa, 1991). The model to account for these, referred to as *problem behavior theory* (Jessor & Jessor, 1977), proposes that problem behaviors cluster together because they serve similar functions in relation to development. Autonomy from parents and bonding with peers are two of the functions that may be served by such behaviors. There has been considerable support for the notion of constellations of antisocial behavior in clinical as well as community samples. Consequently, one approach to the conceptualization of conduct disorder is to consider a broad class or a "general deviance syndrome" that includes a variety of deviant (i.e., conduct problem) behaviors that go together and vary over the course of development (McGee & Newcomb, 1992).

Another proposal that departs from somewhat distinct subtypes considers the progression of type and severity of conduct disorder symptoms over the course of development (Lahey, Loeber, Quay, Frick, & Grimm, 1992; Loeber, Keenan, Lahey, Green, & Thomas, 1993). In this proposal, three levels of conduct disorder are considered—beginning with oppositional symptoms (e.g., stubbornness, temper tantrums), followed by moderately severe conduct problems (e.g., fighting, lying, stealing), and finally more serious conduct problems (e.g., breaking and entering, theft with confrontation). This proposal emphasizes a progression of symptoms from less to more severe and the emergence of these different levels over the course of development. Focusing on levels of severity and on the sequencing of impairment over development captures the continuity of dysfunction. Not everyone progresses from early to later levels, but it is likely that dysfunction is cumulative and

that more severe symptoms are followed by an early history of less severe symptoms (Patterson, 1992).

Needless to say, the different ways of subtyping or characterizing
conduct disorder are not mutually exclusive. Each of the methods mentioned here has supportive data in its behalf, suggesting each is identifying reliable facets of the problem. As a general strategy, it is probably
important to begin with the notion that a number of paths lead to conduct disorder. Subtypes and developmental sequences will identify
some of these paths, but each individual method of subtyping will ex-
clude many youths. Various models raise the prospect of identifying
more of these paths.

ASSESSMENT OF
ANTISOCIAL BEHAVIOR

Diagnosis refers to the different ways of classifying and delineating
disorders. Diagnostic methods rely on some form of measurement. Yet
the purpose of measurement extends well beyond diagnosis. Measurement might be used for multiple goals such as correlating specific
symptom patterns with other characteristics (e.g., school performance,
parent discipline practices) or evaluating the effects of treatment or prevention programs. Assessment can rely on a variety of modalities and
types of measures. Different modalities of assessment, the type of information they yield, and specific measures of conduct disorder will be
discussed.

Modalities of Assessment

Self-Report Measures. Self-report measures of symptoms are frequently used with adult patient samples. Yet children and adolescents
rarely identify themselves as having a "problem" or needing treatment.
Thus one does not necessarily expect to see self-reported dysfunction
with children or adolescents, as one does with adults. Also, the ability
of children to report on their dysfunction is less clear than for adolescents or adults. For these reasons, self-report is less heavily emphasized
in the assessment of childhood disorders than it is for adult disorders.
Adolescents are more likely than children to be administered self-report
measures. They more readily understand what is being asked and can
complete paper-and-pencil measures with little or no assistance. An-

other reason that adolescents are more likely to receive self-report measures pertains to the availability of assessment tools. Measures developed for adults often are used in unmodified form with adolescents.

Although self-report is not usually used as the primary measure to evaluate childhood dysfunction, it can yield important information. Children can report on their symptoms and identify specific problem areas not always evident to their parents. One might expect children to deny conduct problems and hence provide little information of use on self-report measures of antisocial behavior. Yet self-report may be especially valuable for measuring conduct problems that are likely to be concealed from parents. Information regarding such covert behaviors as vandalism, theft, or drug abuse is more readily reported by children and adolescents than by others, or by institutional records (see Elliott, Huizinga, & Ageton, 1985). In general, studies have shown that children can report on their antisocial behavior and readily do so. Age, type of measure, and ways in which information is sought may be relevant to the yield from self-report. However, variations along these dimensions have not been well studied. The validity of self-reported conduct problem behaviors has been attested to in studies showing that they predict subsequent arrest and convictions as well as educational, employment, and marital adjustment (e.g., Bachman et al., 1978; Farrington, 1984).

Reports of Significant Others. Certainly reports of significant others (e.g., parents, teachers, therapists) are the most widely used measures of childhood disorders. Given their obviously unique position to comment on their child's functioning and changes over time, parents are the most frequently relied on source of information. Furthermore, studies have repeatedly shown that parent evaluations of children correlate with clinical judgments of child dysfunction. As an assessment modality, measures completed by significant others have major advantages. Many rating scales are available that can be completed relatively quickly and can cover a wide range of symptom areas. There may be a partial bias in the types of antisocial behaviors that rating scales can assess. Behaviors such as teasing, fighting, yelling, arguing, and other overt acts are likely to be easily detected by parents and teachers. More covert acts, such as stealing, setting fires, substance abuse, and gang behavior, may be more difficult to assess. By their very nature, these latter behaviors are more hidden from the purview of the adult.

Peer Evaluations. Ratings by peers are worth distinguishing even though peers no doubt qualify as "significant others." Also peer measures typically reflect an assessment methodology that departs from the rating scales used for parent and teacher assessments. Peer-based measures usually consist of different ways of soliciting peer nominations of persons who evince particular characteristics (e.g., aggressiveness). The consensus of the peer group is likely to reflect consistencies in performance and stable characteristics. Indeed, elementary school peer evaluations (e.g., measures of dislike or rejection, aggressive behavior) predict conduct problems years later (Coie, Lochman, Terry, & Hyman, 1992; Huesmann et al., 1984).

Peer measures usually consist of sociometric ratings to identify such characteristics as popularity, likeability, acceptance, rejection, and social competence. Such characteristics are quite relevant given the difficulties in each of these areas that antisocial children usually evince. Peer evaluations of social dimensions are correlated with independent evaluations of adjustment. Moreover, peer ratings occasionally are more sensitive as predictors of adjustment than are teacher and clinician ratings.

Direct Observation. A youth's specific behaviors at home, at school, or in the community can be observed directly (see McMahon & Forehand, 1988). The key ingredients of direct observations are defining behavior carefully, identifying the situations in which the behavior will be observed, sending observers to record the behaviors, and ensuring that behavior is observed accurately and reliably. The requirements for direct observation vary as a function of the complexity of the assessment procedures. In clinical research, multiple behaviors are often observed in brief time-intervals while the child interacts with his family at home (e.g., Patterson, 1982). In such cases, highly trained observers are needed to observe behavior. At the other extreme, one or two behaviors (e.g., episodes of stealing or fighting, school attendance) can be assessed at home or at school. With relatively simple observational codes, parents and teachers can be used in place of trained observers.

An advantage of direct observations is that they provide samples of the actual frequency or occurrences of particular antisocial or prosocial behaviors. Thus this modality is distinguished from self-reports and reports of others that can be more influenced by judgments and impressions. Direct observations have their own liabilities. Many behaviors, especially covert acts (e.g., theft, drug use, sexual promiscuity), are not readily observed directly. Also, even when behaviors can be observed, the act of observation can influence their performance. Nevertheless, observation contributes unique information by sampling behaviors directly.

Institutional and Societal Records. Evaluation of antisocial youths frequently relies on institutional records, such as contacts with the police; arrest records; school attendance, grades, graduation, suspensions, and expulsions. Institutional records are exceedingly important because they represent socially significant measures of the impact of the problem. Various governmental agencies at the state and national level monitor such events as the number of juvenile arrests or juvenile court cases. Such information can plot important social trends and facilitate decision making about allocation of resources and services for a particular problem.

There are many problems with institutional and societal records as a measure of antisocial behavior. Most antisocial and delinquent acts are not observed or recorded. In fact, research has suggested that 9 out of 10 illegal acts are not detected or not acted on officially (Empey, 1982). This conclusion has been supported by studies that ask children and adolescents to report on their delinquent and antisocial behaviors (Elliott et al., 1985; Williams & Gold, 1972). Official records can greatly underestimate the incidence of antisocial behaviors because of the slippage between the occurrence of antisocial behavior and the ultimate recording of the act on some archival record. For example, arrest and conviction rates are obviously important but not particularly sensitive measures of delinquent behavior. Most crimes are not detected; those that are only infrequently lead to arrests; those that do lead to arrest are not always referred to the courts; and those that are referred do not necessarily lead to conviction (Empey, 1982).

Notwithstanding these limitations, institutional records are critical measures for the evaluation of antisocial behavior. Antisocial behavior by its very nature leaves its mark on society (e.g., vandalism, firesetting, crime statistics). Institutional records have often been used to measure the behavior of juveniles and to evaluate interventions designed to reduce conduct disorder, as evident in later chapters on treatment and prevention.

General Comments. Each of the modalities discussed has its own strengths, methodological weaknesses, and sources of bias. For example, parent evaluations of deviant child behavior provide an obviously important and unique perspective given that parents usually are in an excellent position to comment on the child's functioning. Yet parent evaluations are influenced by parent stress and psychopathology; they often fail to detect problems identified by child self-report or by direct observation. Similarly, direct observation reflects performance of a particular behavior free from the global judgments and recollections of parents and teachers. Yet the behaviors of interest may be too low in frequency, or they may be performed when observers are not present. Hence direct observation may miss many behaviors of interest. The concerns about any specific assessment modality could be multiplied (see Kazdin, 1992b).

A particular modality may be especially relevant given the specific purposes of assessment. In most instances, multiple modalities should be included in an assessment battery. The reason is that the informational yield and the conclusions that are drawn about the severity or type of dysfunction, the relation of the symptoms to other measures, and changes over time will vary for the different measures.

Selected Examples

Measures of Antisocial Behavior. Several measures are available to assess antisocial and conduct disorder, only a few of which have been well studied. Examples of currently available measures and their salient characteristics are enumerated in Table 2.3. A few measures are highlighted here to focus on characteristics not evident in the table.

Among the self-report measures, no single measure is in widespread use. The *Self-Report Delinquency Scale,* noted in the table, has enjoyed use for children and adolescents beyond the age range for which the scale was originally devised (i.e., ages 11 to 17). This instrument asks the youth directly about the occurrence of delinquent acts at home, at school, and in the community. The items encompass theft, property damage, illegal services (e.g., peddling drugs), public disorder (e.g., making obscene phone calls), status offenses (e.g., running away), and index offenses (e.g., assault). Sometimes select items are omitted (e.g., using checks illegally, threatening others to obtain sex) if they are not relevant to younger children. Items are scored on a 4-point scale with numerical anchors for frequency of occurrence (e.g., 1 = once, 4 = five or more times in the previous year). A *total delinquency score* reflects

TABLE 2.3 Selected Measures of Antisocial Behaviors for Children and Adolescents

Measure	Response Format	Age[a] Range	Special Features
Self-Report			
Children's Action Tendency Scale (Deluty, 1979)	30 items in forced-choice format, child selects what he or she would do in interpersonal situations.	6 to 15 yrs	Scores for response dimensions; agressiveness, assertiveness, and submissiveness.
Adolescent Antisocial Self-Report Behavior Checklist (Kulik, Stein, & Sarbin, 1968)	52 items, each of which is rated by the child on a 5-point scale (from never to very often).	Adolescence	The measure samples a broad range of behaviors from mild misbehavior to serious antisocial acts. The items load four factors: delinquency, drug usage, parental defiance, and assaultiveness.
Self-Report Delinquency Scale (Elliott, Dunford, & Huizinga, 1987)	47 items that measure frequency with which individual has performed offenses included in the Uniform Crime Reports. Responses provide frequency with which behavior was performed over the last year.	11 to 21 yrs	Measure has been developed as part of the National Youth Survey, an extensive longitudinal study of delinquent behavior, alcohol and drug use, and related problems in American youths.
Minnesota Multiphasic Personality Inventory Scales (Lefkowitz, Eron, Walder, & Huesmann, 1977)	True-false items derived from Scales F (test-taking attitude), 4 (psychopathic deviate), and 9 (hypomania) are summed to yield an aggression/delinquency score.	Adolescence	Part of more general measure that assesses multiple areas of psychopathology.

(continued)

39

TABLE 2.3 Continued

Measure	Response Format	Age[a] Range	Special Features
Interview for Aggression[b] (Kazdin & Esveldt-Dawson, 1986)	Semistructured interview, 30 items pertaining to aggression such as getting into fights, starting arguments. Each item rated on a 5-point scale for severity and a 3-point scale for duration.	6 to 13 yrs	Yields scores for severity, duration, and total (severity + duration) aggression. Separate factors assess overt and covert behaviors.
Children's Hostility Inventory[b] (Kazdin, Rodgers, Colbus, & Siegel, 1987)	38 true-false statements assessing different facets of aggression and hostility.	6 to 13 yrs	Derived from Buss-Durke Hostility Guilt Inventory. A priori subscales from that scale comprise factors that relate to overt acts (aggression) and aggressive thoughts and feelings (hostility).
Reports of Others			
Eyberg Child Behavior Inventory (Eyberg & Robinson, 1983)	36 items rated on 1- to 7-point scale for frequency and whether the behavior is a problem.	2 to 17 yrs	Designed to measure wide range of conduct problems in the home.
Sutter-Eyberg Student Behavior Inventory (Funderbunk & Eyberg, 1989)	36 items identical in format but not content to the Eyberg Child Behavior Inventory.	2 to 17 yrs	Measures a range of conduct problem behaviors at school.
Peer Nomination of Aggression (Lefkowitz et al., 1977)	Items that ask children to nominate others who show the characteristics (e.g., "Who starts a fight over nothing?")	3rd through 13th grade	Items reflect the child's reputation among peers regarding overall aggression. Different versions of peer nominations have been used.

Direct Observations

Measure	Age[a]	Description	Comments
Adolescent Antisocial Behavioral Checklist (Curtiss et al., 1983)	Adolescence	57 items to measure antisocial behavior during hospitalization. Behaviors are rated as having occurred or not based on staff observations.	The items can be scored using different sets of subscales; one set focuses on the form of the problem (e.g., physical vs. verbal harm); another set focuses on the objects of aggression (e.g., toward self, others, property). Different versions are available and differ in scoring.
Family Interaction Coding System (Reid, 1978)	3 to 12 yrs	Direct observational system to measure occurrence or nonoccurrence of 29 specific parent-child behaviors in the home. Each behavior is scored within small intervals for an hour each day for a period of several days.	Individual behaviors are observed but usually summarized with a total aversive behavior score. The general procedure can be adopted using some or all of the behaviors of the FICS.
Parent Daily Report (Chamberlain & Reid, 1987)	3 to 12 yrs	Parents identify symptoms of antisocial behavior. After symptoms are identified, the parent is called daily for several days. Each day the parent is asked if each behavior has or has not occurred in previous 24-hour period.	Measure does not reflect a standardized set of items but rather refers more to an assessment approach for collecting data on behaviors at home.

a. The age ranges are tentative and are derived from age of cases reported rather than inherent restrictions of the measure.
b. This measure has two separate versions: a self-report measure for children, and a parent-report measure to evaluate children's behavior.

41

severity of delinquent behavior; subscale scores are available for different types of illegal activity that may be of interest as well.

Measures completed by significant others have received more attention than self-report measures. A prime example is the frequently used and extensively evaluated *Eyberg Child Behavior Inventory* (ECBI) (Eyberg & Robinson, 1983; Robinson, Eyberg, & Ross, 1980). The measure is used to assess child behavior problems that parents report at home. Sample items include verbally fighting with friends one's own age, refusing to do chores when asked, poor table manners, and yelling or screaming. Most of the items reflect refusal and other oppositional behaviors that are annoying to parents, rather than serious antisocial acts. However, there are exceptions (e.g., stealing, destroying objects). Each item is rated by the parent as to whether it is a problem (yes, no) and how often it occurs (1 = never to 7 = always). The measure yields two scores that reflect the number of problems (i.e., those items endorsed affirmatively) and the intensity of problems (i.e., a total of the scale scores summed for all items).

As an illustration of direct observational methods, the *Family Interaction Coding System* (FICS) (see Reid, Baldwin, Patterson, & Dishion, 1988) warrants special mention. The FICS has been used to record behaviors of antisocial children as they interact with their parents and siblings at home. More specifically, the measure is designed to assess aggressive behaviors and the antecedents and consequences (family interactions) with which they are associated. Among direct observation systems, the FICS is relatively elaborate. Twenty-nine different behaviors are coded by observers as present or absent in each of several brief time intervals (e.g., 30 seconds) over a period of approximately 1 hour. Prosocial and deviant child behaviors (e.g., complying with requests, attacking someone, yelling) and parent behaviors (e.g., providing approval, playing with the child, humiliating the child) are included.

The FICS has several important requirements. First, observers must be carefully trained and closely monitored to ensure that the codes are scored reliably. Second, the situations in which observers complete their assessment need to be partially controlled to limit the variability in the setting. For example, when the FICS is used in the home, families are instructed to remain in a small number of rooms during the period when observations are obtained. Families may not watch television or make outgoing phone calls. All of these restrictions help observers in scoring child-parent interactions. The FICS and other less complex direct observational codes have been used frequently to assess antisocial behaviors at home and at school (McMahon & Forehand, 1988).

Overall, relatively few measures developed for antisocial behavior among children and adolescents have been in widespread use. Typically, measures have been devised and used for a specific purpose as part of an ongoing research program. With few exceptions, little validational work has been conducted, nor have data been provided to indicate the normative levels of antisocial behavior on the measure over the course of development.

General Measures of Psychopathology. Most studies of antisocial behavior rely on measures that assess diverse areas of psychopathology and functioning. The reasons are manifold: To begin, such measures provide information about the domain of interest and many other areas as well. This feature is important because children who suffer antisocial behavior may also show dysfunction in other areas (e.g., hyperactivity, anxiety). In addition, general measures of psychopathology offer a number of parent and teacher rating scales that have been well researched and validated.

Different types of measures are available that assess a broad range of symptoms and behaviors. *Diagnostic interviews* are used in assessing dysfunction among children and adolescents. In such interviews, parent and child typically are interviewed (separately) to evaluate the presence and/or severity of the full range of symptoms. The goal is to permit the examiner to provide a diagnosis based on a specific diagnostic system, usually *DSM-III-R* or more recently *DSM-IV*. Several diagnostic interviews are available (e.g., *Diagnostic Interview Schedule for Children, Schedule for Affective Disorders and Schizophrenia for School-Age Children*, the *Diagnostic Interview for Children and Adolescents*, and the *Child Assessment Schedule;* see Hodges & Zeman, 1993).

The best developed measures that assess multiple areas of child and adolescent dysfunction are *parent and teacher rating scales.* Typically these scales present a large number of items that the parent or teacher rates in terms of presence or absence or severity of dysfunction. The *Child Behavior Checklist* (CBCL; Achenbach, 1991) is typical of an instrument for parents to rate items conveying characteristics of their children. The measure includes 118 items that refer to behavior problems, each of which is rated on a 3-point scale (0 = not true, 2 = very or often true). Three sample items include cruelty, bullying, or meanness to others; argues a lot; and sets fires. The scale yields several different factors or constellations of symptoms, including aggression, delinquency, hyperactivity, anxiety, depression, uncommunicativeness, schizophrenia, and others. The scale has been evaluated separately for different age groups (i.e., 4 to 11 and 12 to 18 years) and for clinic and community (nonreferred) samples. Consequently, with the CBCL, one can evaluate an individual child's standing on all the symptom scales or factors relative to same age and gender peers who have not been referred for treatment. Many other rating scales and checklists have been administered to parents. Prominent examples include the *Behavior Problem Checklist,* the *Parent Symptom Questionnaire,* the *Louisville Behavior Checklist,* the *Institute for Juvenile Research Behavior Checklist,* and the *Personality Inventory for Children* (see Barkley, 1988; McConaughy, 1992).

Teacher evaluations of child behavior also play a role in identification of childhood dysfunction. Teachers observe children for protracted amounts of time and across a wide range of situations (e.g., structured vs. unstructured classroom activities; academic, social, and recreational settings). Moreover, the teacher can evaluate children in the context of their peers. A given child's departure from his or her peers provides a perspective that may not be available to parents. Teacher and parent rating instruments usually do not differ in structure or format. Indeed, many scales such as the *Behavior Problem Checklist* have been administered to parents, teachers, and other adults (e.g., clinic staff). For other measures, parallel forms exist for teacher and parents. Examples include the *CBCL-Teacher Report Form,* the *Conners Teachers Questionnaire,* and the *School Behavior Checklist,* which are parallel to the forms mentioned earlier for parents (see Barkley, 1988; McConaughy, 1992).

As an assessment modality, parent and teacher rating scales have been widely used. Their value derives from sampling a wide spectrum of symptom areas and from their ease of administration. Considerable data have been generated on their use and psychometric properties (e.g., reliability and validity). Also, for many measures, normative data are available permitting comparison of clinic and nonclinic samples and of variations in symptom areas as a function of age, gender, social class, and other subject or demographic variables.

CURRENT ISSUES AND LIMITATIONS

Delineation of Conduct Disorder

Advances have been made in the diagnosis of conduct disorder and other disorders more generally. For example, in the fourth edition of the *DSM*, criteria for invoking diagnoses have been better specified than in previous editions. Nevertheless, there is still a lack of *operational criteria* denoting specific measurement strategies and cutoff scores for identifying diagnostic groups. Thus it has not been worked out exactly how to measure conduct disorder. Diagnostic interviews are used to reach formal diagnoses, but the point at which a conduct problem is delineated as a "symptom" is not well anchored by specific criteria.

In contemporary research, the identification of conduct disorder has been inconsistent. For example, relatively high scores on specific parent rating scales (e.g., the externalizing scale of the CBCL), clinical diagnoses obtained informally from an unstructured interview or a review of institutional records, referrals from teachers of children who are "behavioral problems," and parental responses to advertisements to recruit children who are unmanageable all have been used to identify conduct disorder children. It is very likely that some children selected by any of these procedures would meet diagnostic criteria (e.g., *DSM-IV*) for Conduct Disorder.

Even if all children within a given sample meet criteria for the diagnosis of Conduct Disorder, that by itself does not mean that the sample is homogenous. The diagnosis requires only a small number of symptoms (3) from a much larger set. Conduct Disorder youths may vary in the symptoms they show; two youths with nonoverlapping sets of symptoms might still receive the same diagnosis. Diagnosis is useful to begin the process of research to address these matters but fundamental questions remain. Already mentioned was the overlap of diagnoses (Conduct Disorder with Oppositional Defiant Disorder and Attention-Deficit/Hyperactivity Disorder) highlighting further the need to view the current system as tentative. The importance of carefully assessing youths and the full range of their emotional and behavioral characteristics is underscored by diagnostic dilemmas. Careful assessment provides the basis for developing the most useful way to delineate different symptom patterns.

In much of the work on antisocial behavior, assessment procedures do not permit careful delineation of the sample. Whether antisocial behaviors are present, severe, or primary as a presenting problem, or whether the children are "overactive" and therefore bothersome to teachers, parents, or both is not easily discerned. The ambiguous and inconsistent identification of samples for clinical research makes it difficult to know the characteristics of a particular sample and to compare different samples (across studies).

In general, it is important to develop further criteria that will be used to define conduct disorder and the manner in which these criteria will be assessed. To make further advances, there need not be agreement on the many complex questions such as the subtypes of conduct disorder and the organization of symptom patterns. Rather these questions can be better served by attempts to use standardized measures and explicit criteria to select samples for further research.

Convergence of Different Measures

As a more general problem, diverse measures of child behavior (e.g., parent, teacher, and self-report ratings and direct observations) may show little or no correlation. For example, there is little or no agreement between parents and children when they each complete the identical measure to assess antisocial child behavior or other dysfunctions (see Achenbach, McConaughy, & Howell, 1987; Kazdin, 1994). Many behaviors, particularly antisocial behaviors (e.g., setting fires, stealing, running away, breaking school rules, trying to kill someone), are not as likely to be perceived *as a problem* by children as they are by parents. In general, the lack of agreement among different sources of information regarding child symptoms seems to be a function of the source of information (e.g., mother, father, child), different perspectives (e.g., parents, teachers, mental health workers), and the types of behavior (e.g., subjective vs. overt signs).

Different assessment modalities imperfectly measure the behaviors of interest and are influenced by multiple factors. For example, noted already were the findings that parent report of deviant child behavior depends on the parent's stress and symptoms of psychopathology (especially depression and anxiety), marital discord, expectations of child behavior, parent self-esteem, and reported stress in the home (see Kazdin, 1994). Greater parent stress and dysfunction are associated with rating the child as more deviant. Thus parent's check marks on a rating scale measure their own dysfunction in part as well as that of the child. This does not gainsay the concurrent and predictive value of parental measures but tempers the interpretation of what they reflect.

At present there is no simple way to determine which measure reflects "true" performance. The lack of "objective" criteria against which to calibrate diverse measures makes it difficult to evaluate a given measurement technique. Some attempts have been made to validate different measures against direct observation of overt behavior. Discrepancies between parent or teacher reports and measures of overt behavior are common. However, direct observations raise their own problems. They do not always sample broadly across behaviors or situations, and their specific codes may not reflect the salience or significance of the symptom (e.g., for low frequency but highly significant behaviors such as setting fires or stealing). Although direct observations may provide concrete and clear criteria for scoring behavior, no single measure or method of assessment provides a flawless criterion against which other measures can be validated. Consequently, multiple measures are used to identify different facets and perspectives in clinical evaluation and in research on conduct disorder.

General Comments

There are many ambiguities in both diagnosis and assessment of conduct disorder. The overlap of diagnoses such as Conduct Disorder and Attention-Deficit/Hyperactivity Disorder and the lack of operational criteria are especially important to bear in mind when reference is made to Conduct Disorder. The multiple assessment methods and their different results in regard to the characteristics of a particular child also raise ambiguities. Ratings from different sources (e.g., child, parent, teacher) provide valid information that correlates with other criteria. However, these sources may show little correlation with each other. There is, at present, no objective measure of conduct disorder that is free of some source of bias, artifact, or judgment. The use of several different measures is essential to overcome the limitations of any single modality or scale.

The discussion has focused on the assessment of antisocial behavior and various measures that might be used toward that end. Yet conduct disorder in children and adolescents is associated with a wide range of other characteristics that may be of interest for assessment purposes. For example, among conduct problem youths, measures of cognitive processes, social skills, and academic functioning are obvious areas that come to mind. The child's behavior in each of these, and related areas, may be as important and as dysfunctional as the specific antisocial behaviors that may have served as the basis for referral. Similarly, because of the strong association of family variables with childhood antisocial behavior, measures of marital discord, parent psychopathology, and life events are relevant as well. Given the pervasiveness of child, parent, and family dysfunction in severe cases of antisocial behavior, it is difficult to delimit the relevant measures to a circumscribed set.

SUMMARY AND CONCLUSIONS

The present chapter described current diagnosis criteria for Conduct Disorder (as reflected in *DSM-IV*) as well as other disorders in which antisocial behaviors may emerge as predominant symptoms. In general, the specific criteria used to reach a diagnosis can be argued. The fact that the criteria change over time as a given system (e.g., *DSM*) is revised and that they vary between separate systems at a given time (e.g., *DSM-IV* vs. *ICD-10*) means that the criteria must be viewed as tentative. Patterns of conduct problems do emerge. This chapter discussed variations in these patterns as a function of sex and age.

Research designed to identify subtypes is a means to bring order to the very heterogeneous youths who show conduct problems. Major lines of research have suggested subtypes based on aggressive and delinquent behavior, aggressors and stealers, overt and covert behavior, and child and adolescent onset of symptoms, to mention a few. Perhaps the best supported distinction is between aggressive and delinquent types. However, as we have seen, these types may encompass other types as well (e.g., aggressive type includes overt problems more likely with a child onset). Clearly, there is sufficient heterogeneity within the subtypes proposed to conclude that research is at an early stage.

The assessment of antisocial behavior has relied on a number of measures, including interviews, self-report, parent, teacher, and peer ratings, direct observations, and institutional records. The kinds of information such measures provide and the interpretive problems they raise were identified briefly. Diagnosis and assessment are fundamental to research that is designed to understand the nature of antisocial behavior, its causes, correlates, and clinical course. Measures that apply to diverse disorders of childhood and adolescence have received a great deal of attention and are relatively well developed. In contrast, there remains a need to develop measures that focus exclusively on the broad range of antisocial behaviors. Such measures can elaborate the range of behaviors and perhaps identify subtypes of antisocial behavior that will have important implications for early detection, prevention, and treatment.

NOTES

1. Two general diagnostic approaches are often distinguished and include the more commonly used categorical approach (discussed here) and the dimensional approach. A dimensional approach is designed to evaluate the degree to which individuals show various characteristics such as individual symptoms or symptom patterns. A discussion of these different approaches toward diagnosis and their interrelation is beyond the scope of the present chapter (see Achenbach, 1993a; Blashfield, 1984).

2. The identification of a disorder or disorders is one task of current diagnosis using the *DSM*. Diagnosis addresses multiple axes or domains of information including the presence of clinical disorders or conditions that warrant attention (Axis I), personality disorders or mental retardation (Axis II), relevant medical conditions (Axis III), psychosocial and environmental problems (Axis IV), and overall functioning in everyday life (Axis V) (APA, 1994).

3

RISK FACTORS, ONSET, AND COURSE OF DYSFUNCTION

Conduct disorder does not merely emerge spontaneously, nor is its emergence random in a nonselected set of individuals in a population. The question to which one is immediately drawn is, "What is the *cause* of conduct disorder?" The question conveys somewhat simplistic thinking about the problem. Current research is not driven by the search for a simple or single cause of conduct disorder. The complexity of human behavior, the range of influences (e.g., biological, psychological, and sociological), and the heterogeneity of behaviors encompassed by conduct disorder preclude simple answers.

Current work tends to focus on factors that influence the likelihood that a particular outcome (such as conduct disorder) will occur. Rather than causing a particular outcome in some deterministic fashion, the factors operate to increase or decrease the probability of that outcome. Implied in this view is that no single event leads to conduct disorder. There are multiple paths and influences that can lead to the outcome. A few key concepts are worth noting insofar as they reflect how influences on outcomes such as conduct disorder are conceptualized and investigated.

Risk factors are characteristics, events, or processes that increase the likelihood (or risk) for the onset of a problem or dysfunction (e.g., conduct disorder). We are already familiar with risk factors in general because these are discussed in the media in varying contexts. For example, we know that high cholesterol, sedentary lifestyle, cigarette smoking, and stress (e.g., perhaps from reading articles about risk factors) increase the risk for heart disease. A notion related to risk factors is *vulnerability* or the susceptibility to a particular outcome. Whatever else risk factors do, they make an individual more vulnerable. Vulnerability entails the reduced capacity to ward off other influences. *Protective factors* refer to characteristics, events, or processes that decrease the impact of a risk factor. Individuals may be exposed to a set of risk factors while other influences may attenuate or reduce the impact of these risk factors. Discussions of protective factors focus on the concept of *resilience*, which is the counterpart of vulnerability. Resilience refers to the capacity to adapt positively in the face of deleterious influences. Efforts to understand the unfolding of dysfunction emphasize risk and protective factors. More attention has been accorded risk factors in relation to child and adolescent dysfunction in general; that emphasis will be reflected in this chapter.

RISK FACTORS FOR THE
ONSET OF CONDUCT DISORDER

The factors that predispose children and adolescents to conduct disorder have been studied extensively in the context of clinical referrals and adjudicated delinquents (see Henggeler, 1989; Patterson, Reid, & Dishion, 1992; Robins & Rutter, 1990). The list of factors that have been implicated is quite long. Major categories include factors related to the child, the parent and family, and the school.

Child Factors

Child Temperament. Temperament refers to those prevailing aspects of personality showing some consistency across situations and time. The basis for these characteristics is considered to be genetic or constitutional, a view attributed in part to the fact that differences can be identified among children very early in life. Differences in temperament are often based on such characteristics as activity levels, emotional responsiveness, quality of moods, and social adaptability. For example, one dimension of temperament used to distinguish children is "easy-to-difficult" (Plomin, 1983). "Easy" children are characterized by positive mood, approach toward new stimuli, adaptability to change, and low intensity reactions to new stimuli. "Difficult" children, who show opposite patterns on the above characteristics, are likely to show behavioral problems concurrently or to develop these problems later (e.g., Reitsma-Street, Offord, & Finch, 1985). Difficult children are also more likely to be referred for treatment for aggressive behaviors and tantrums (Rutter, Birch, Thomas, & Chess, 1964).

Neuropsychological Deficits and Difficulties. Neuropsychological deficits and difficulties refer to diverse aspects of functioning that reflect central nervous system functioning and affect a variety of specific domains of performance. The domains include abilities such as cognitive processes, language and speech, motor coordination, impulsivity, attention, mental abilities (e.g., intelligence). From a neuropsychological perspective, these processes are studied insofar as they reflect brain functioning and development.

Evidence suggests that neurological deficits and difficulties early in life place a youth at risk for subsequent conduct problems and delinquency (Moffitt, 1993a, 1993b). Many such deficits and difficulties have been identified using standardized neuropsychological measures. For example, deficits in diverse functions related to language (e.g., verbal learning, verbal fluency, verbal IQ), memory, motor coordination, integration of auditory and visual cues, and "executive" functions of the brain (e.g., abstract reasoning, concept formation, planning, control of attention) are among the factors shown to predict subsequent conduct disorder. These and related dysfunctions are of interest because many measures are considered to reflect functioning of specific structures of the brain and therefore to suggest possible neurological underpinnings of conduct disorder. Also, neurological impairment may reflect, and hence partially explain, the impact on child behavior of other influences, such as pre- and postnatal exposure to toxic agents (e.g., maternal drug abuse, poor maternal nutrition, exposure to lead). The more salient issue to note is that early neuropsychological dysfunctions predict subsequent conduct disorder (e.g., in adolescence and adulthood).

Subclinical Levels of Conduct Disorder. Several studies have found that subclinical levels of conduct disorder predict later conduct disorder (Farrington, 1991; Loeber, 1990). Teacher and peer measures of aggressiveness and unmanageability early or late in the school years predict subsequent conduct disorder. These behaviors can be called "subclinical" levels because they are not of the severity that leads to clinical referral. Although there is a clear continuity of problematic behavior, this does not mean that all, or indeed even most, youths with obstreperous behavior are identified later as antisocial. Nonetheless, early child behavior is one of the more robust predictors of later conduct disorder.

It is more than the mere presence of unmanageable behavior that serves as a risk factor. Age of onset, number of different types of antisocial behaviors, and number of situations in which the antisocial behaviors are evident (e.g., at home, school, the community) are relevant as well (Loeber, 1990). Children with earlier onset and greater diversity of problems are at greater risk.

Academic and Intellectual Performance. Academic deficiencies and lower levels of intellectual functioning are associated with conduct disorder. This relation has been demonstrated with diverse measures of intellectual and school performance (e.g., verbal and nonverbal intelligence tests, grades, achievement tests) and measures of conduct disorder (e.g., youth self-report, teacher report, official records of delinquency) (see Rutter & Giller, 1983; West, 1982). Of course, the association does not necessarily mean that academic dysfunction represents a risk factor. Reduced time at school (e.g., truancy, expulsion) and less attention from teachers might lead to poor academic achievement. However, evidence suggests that academic deficiencies and lower IQ often predict subsequent conduct disorder (e.g., Farrington, 1991; Moffitt, 1993a).

Academic and intellectual functioning are known to relate to other variables such as socioeconomic class and family size. Even when these variables are controlled, educational and intellectual functioning serve as predictors of conduct disorder (West, 1982). Although academic dysfunction is a risk factor for subsequent conduct disorder, the relation is not merely unidirectional. Conduct disorder predicts subsequent failure at school and lower level of educational attainment (Bachman et al., 1978; Ledingham & Schwartzman, 1984).

Parent and Family Factors

Genetic Loading. Several lines of evidence have emerged in support of the role of the genetic factors in placing individuals at risk (see DiLalla & Gottesman, 1989). Twin studies are frequently used to demonstrate the role of genetic influences because monozygotic twins are, of course, much more similar genetically than dizygotic twins (or siblings). In twin studies, higher concordance rates (i.e., the likelihood that the other twin has the disorder if one twin does) among monozygotic versus dizygotic twins would be consistent with genetic transmission. Such studies have shown greater concordance of delinquency, criminality, and conduct disorder among monozygotic versus dizygotic twins. In studies of adult criminality, the genetic evidence is rather strong: Concordance is more than twice as great among monozygotic twins compared with dizygotic twins (Gottesman, Carey, & Hanson, 1983). Studies of adolescent youths have indicated that the concordance rates for delinquency among monozygotic and dizygotic twins is 87% and 72%, respectively (see Plomin, 1991). This suggests a genetic influence in adolescence but not a strong influence, because the rate is only slightly higher for monozygotic twins.

Attribution of the differences in concordance between monozygotic and dizygotic twins to genetic factors assumes that the environments for the different types of twins are equated. Yet environmental factors may be more similar for monozygotic than for dizygotic twins, because parents of monozygotic twins may treat them more alike. Adoption studies better separate genetic and environmental influences because the child often is separated from the biological parent at birth. With adoption very early in life, subsequent similarities in parent and child behavior cannot be attributed to the biological parent's child-rearing practices and related interpersonal influences.

Adoption studies have shown that conduct disorder and criminality in offspring are more likely when the biological relative has shown these behaviors (Cadoret, 1978; Crowe, 1974). This finding establishes the role of genetics in contributing to the emergence of conduct disorder. Yet genetic factors alone cannot account for current findings. Adoption studies have also affirmed the influence of such environmental factors as adverse conditions in the home (e.g., marital discord, psychiatric dysfunction), exposure to discontinuous mothering before being placed in the final adoptive setting, and the age at which the child has been adopted (Cadoret & Cain, 1981). This work suggests the combined role of genetic and environmental factors. The dual contribution of genetic and environmental influences can be seen in studies showing that conduct disorder in both the biological and the adoptive parent increases the risk of conduct disorder in the child (see Brennan, Mednick, & Kandel, 1991), although the impact of the biological parent is much greater. Yet the risk is greatly increased when both genetic and environmental influences are present (e.g., Cadoret, Cain, & Crowe, 1983).

In general, the evidence for a genetic influence appears to be better established and stronger for conduct disorder in adults than in children and adolescents. However, insufficient research has been conducted to be able to state that the genetic influence is necessarily less in childhood than in adulthood (see Frick & Jackson, 1993). Perhaps the genetic influence in adolescents might be less than in childhood and adulthood. In adolescence, many youths engage in conduct disorder behaviors, but do not continue these behaviors in adulthood. The increase in such behaviors may be less of an underlying pattern and less readily attributed to genetic influences, except for the subgroup of those who continue the pattern into adulthood.

Psychopathology and Criminal Behavior in the Family. Psychopathology in the parents places the child at risk for psychological dysfunction in general (Rutter et al., 1970; Werner & Smith, 1992). As might be expected, the risk for conduct disorder in the child is more specifically related to the presence of related dysfunction in either parent. Criminal behavior, antisocial personality disorder, and alcoholism increase the child's risk for conduct disorder (Rutter & Giller, 1983; West & Prinz, 1987). For example, children with alcoholic parents have more contact with police, more substance abuse, and higher rates of truancy and dropping out of school.

Most studies of parental dysfunction have focused on the parents of the conduct disorder child. Grandparents of antisocial children and adolescents, on both paternal and maternal sides, are more likely to show conduct disorder (i.e., criminal behavior and alcoholism) than are grandparents of youths who are not antisocial (Glueck & Glueck, 1968). Longitudinal studies have shown that aggressive behavior is stable across generations within a family. More specific statements can be made. For example, a good predictor of how aggressive the child will be is the level of aggression of the father at about the same age (Huesmann et al., 1984). In general, a history of antisocial or aggressive behavior in one's family places a child at risk for these behaviors.

Parent-Child Interaction. Several features related to the interaction of parents with their children are risk factors for conduct disorder. Parent disciplinary practices and attitudes have been especially well studied. It has been known for some time that the degree of child aggression in nonclinic populations is related to severity of punishment in the home (Sears, Maccoby, & Levin, 1957). Punishment practices often are extreme in the homes of conduct disorder youths. Indeed, such parents tend to be harsh in their attitudes and disciplinary practices with their children (see Farrington, 1978; Kazdin, 1985). Conduct disorder youths are more likely than both nonreferred youths and clinical referrals without conduct disorder to be victims of child abuse and to be in homes where spouse abuse is evident (Widom, 1989).

Apart from harsh punishment, studies have shown that more lax, erratic, and inconsistent discipline practices within a given parent, and between the parents, are related to delinquency. For example, severity of punishment on the part of the father and lax discipline on the part of the mother have been implicated in later delinquent behavior. When parents are consistent in their discipline practices, even if they are punitive, children are less likely to be at risk for delinquency (McCord, McCord, & Zola, 1959). Although severity and consistency of punishment contribute to aggressive behavior (Patterson et al., 1992), some evidence suggests that parent punishment may be a response to child aggression rather than an antecedent to it (Eron, Huesmann, & Zelli, 1991). It is likely that parents respond to annoying and deviant behavior of the child and in the process inadvertently exacerbate the child's deviant and then aggressive behavior. The relation between child deviance and punishment is likely to be that each begets and promotes the other, and, in the process, they both become more extreme.

Apart from punishment practices, research suggests that the other ways of controlling child behavior are problematic among parents of antisocial youths. Parents of antisocial children are more likely to give commands to their children, to reward deviant behavior directly through attention and compliance, and to ignore or provide aversive consequences for prosocial behavior (Patterson et al., 1992). Fine-grained analyses of parent-child interactions suggest that antisocial behavior, particularly aggression, is systematically, albeit unwittingly, trained in the homes of antisocial children.

Supervision of the child, as another aspect of parent-child contact, has been frequently implicated in conduct disorder (Glueck & Glueck, 1968; Robins, 1966). Parents of antisocial or delinquent children are less likely to monitor their children's whereabouts or to make arrangements for their children's care when they are temporarily away from the home. Other factors considered to reflect poor supervision and to constitute risk factors include not having rules in the home stating where the children can go and when they must return home, allowing children to roam the streets, and permitting the children to engage in many independent and unsupervised activities (Wilson, 1980).

Features that reflect the quality of parent-child and family relationships also serve as risk factors. Parents of antisocial youths, compared with parents of nonreferred youths, show less acceptance of their children, less warmth, affection, and emotional support, and they report less attachment (see Henggeler, 1989). At the level of family relations, less supportive and more defensive communications among family members, less participation in activities as a family, and more clear dominance of one family member also distinguish families of youths with conduct disorder.

Parental Separation, Divorce, and Marital Discord. Separation from one or both parents may be due to several factors, such as parental death, institutionalization, and divorce. In general, separation during childhood increases risk of psychiatric impairment from a variety of childhood disorders (Rutter et al., 1970). In relation to conduct disorder, research has consistently demonstrated that unhappy marital relationships, interpersonal conflicts, and aggression characterize the parental relations of delinquent and antisocial children (Rutter & Giller, 1983). Whether or not the parents are separated, it is the extent of discord and overt conflict that is associated with the risk for conduct disorder and childhood dysfunction (Hetherington, Cox, & Cox, 1982). More extreme open conflict is evident in physical abuse between parents; viewing such violence increases the likelihood that children will be violent themselves (Jaffe, Hurley, & Wolfe, 1990).

Birth Order and Family Size. Birth order is related to the onset of conduct disorder. Conduct disorder is greater among middle children in comparison to only children, first born, or youngest children (e.g., Glueck & Glueck, 1968; McCord et al., 1959), although there are some exceptions (e.g., Eron et al., 1991). The effects are complex and, in the case of delinquency, may vary as a function of type of offense and duration of the only-child status (e.g., length of time before a sibling is born). However, in general, an extended period of time as the only or the youngest child before the sibling is born reduces risk for delinquency.

Larger family size (i.e., more children in the family) increases risk of delinquency (Glueck & Glueck, 1968). Family size obviously relates to findings of birth order. Efforts to separate these factors have examined family size and the birth spacing of offspring. Children with older siblings are more likely to be delinquent; the older the siblings (i.e., the greater the space in age between them), the greater the likelihood of delinquency (Wadsworth, 1979). Interestingly, the risk is associated with the number of brothers (rather than sisters) in the family (Offord, 1982). If one of the brothers is antisocial, the others are at increased risk for conduct disorder.

Socioeconomic Disadvantage. Poverty, overcrowding, unemployment, receipt of social assistance ("welfare"), and poor housing are among the salient measures of socioeconomic disadvantage that increase risk for conduct disorder and delinquency (Hawkins, Catalano, & Miller, 1992). The effects appear to be enduring. For example, low income in childhood predicts adult criminal behavior 30 years later (Kolvin, Miller, Fleeting, & Kolvin, 1988). Interpretation of the impact of low income and related indices of disadvantage is complicated by the association of social class with many other known risk factors, such as large family size, overcrowding, and poor child supervision, among others. When these separate factors are controlled, social disadvantage by itself does not always show a relation to conduct disorder (Robins, 1978; Wadsworth, 1979). Also, it is likely that socioeconomic disadvantage exacerbates other factors. For example, limited financial resources can decrease the likelihood of child supervision (e.g., hiring baby-sitters) and increase stress (e.g., inability to repair an automobile and the attendant inconveniences). In general, socioeconomic disadvantage can be viewed as a risk factor. However, once all other associated features are controlled, the precise role of economic issues is not always evaluated.

School-Related Factors

Characteristics of the Setting. The school setting has been studied as contributing to the risk of conduct disorder. Schools can be characterized in many ways, including their organization, locale, teacher-student ratio, and other characteristics. However, many of these characteristics are difficult to separate from each other and from characteristics of the students and families that the schools serve. For example, schools in some areas of a city may have a higher proportion of families who live in poverty, use harsh child-rearing practices, and provide poor child supervision. These latter factors, rather than the school conditions, might account for the greater risk of the children. Even with such complexities taken into account, characteristics of the schools seem to place youths at risk for conduct disorder.

Rutter and his colleagues (Rutter, Maughan, Mortimore, & Ouston, 1979) examined 12 different secondary schools and their association with child behavior outcomes, including attendance, continuation in school, delinquency rates, and academic performance. Several characteristics of the schools influenced more favorable outcomes. These included an emphasis on academic work, teacher time spent on lessons, teacher use of praise and appreciation for school work, emphasis on individual responsibility of the students, good working conditions for pupils (e.g., clean classroom, furniture in good repair), availability of the teacher to deal with children's problems, and consistent teacher expectations. The overall findings indicated reliable differences among schools on the outcome measures that could not be accounted for simply by differences in physical characteristics of the schools (i.e., size, available space) or by the different types of children and families within the schools. Moreover, the data suggested that the combination of several factors, rather than any single variable, contributed to more favorable child outcomes. In any case, characteristics of the school may contribute to, and increase the risk for, conduct disorder.

Other Factors

The child, parent, and family factors reviewed previously are generally regarded as the most robust predictors of conduct disorder (Loeber, 1990; Rutter & Giller, 1983; Yoshikawa, 1994). Yet within these domains, the above list is incomplete. For example, additional parent and family risk factors could be identified, such as mental retardation of the parent, teen pregnancy, early marriage of the parents, lack of parent interest in the child's school performance, and lack of participation of the family in religious or recreational activities.

Additional domains of risk might be included as well. For example, perinatal and prenatal complications (e.g., maternal infection, prematurity and low birth weight, impaired respiration at birth, and minor birth injury) increase the risk for antisocial and delinquent behavior (Werner & Smith, 1982). Chronic illness in childhood and damage to the central nervous system (i.e., during birth) also increase risk for conduct disorder (see Mrazek & Haggerty, 1994). Other influences (e.g., exposure to violent and aggressive television in childhood) also increase the risk for aggressive behavior over the course of adolescence and adulthood (Lefkowitz, Eron, Walder, & Huesmann, 1977). The role of television has been especially well studied; other media that portray violence (e.g., movies, videogames) also appear to increase risk of conduct problems (see Strasburger, 1995).

Research suggests a dazzling array of risk factors. Which are the most important and how do all of the factors operate? Perhaps the best supported conclusion to date is that the accumulation of risk factors increases the risk for clinical dysfunction (see Rutter & Giller, 1983; Yoshikawa, 1994). The way in which risk factors accumulate and affect the outcome (i.e., conduct disorder) warrants comment. The presence of a single risk factor may not increase risk, either at all or at least very much. When a small number of risk factors are present, risk accelerates; when more are added, the risk goes up several times more. In short, as factors begin to accumulate, the risk is not linear, but rather climbs steeply. Stated another way, youths with four risk factors do not show twice the risk of youths with two factors; instead, they are at several times greater risk for conduct disorder. In clinical samples, typically youths show many risk factors (e.g., in our clinic 8 to 10 of the above risk factors are quite common). Although the number of factors is critical, of course, some factors contribute to risk more than others. Parent psychiatric disorder, parent discipline practices, and economic disadvantage are sometimes among the more salient factors. Yet the complexities in evaluating risk factors, discussed next, make conclusions about *the* most salient subset of factors difficult to reach.

Complexities in Evaluating Risk Factors

It is useful to enumerate risk factors individually to convey their relation to the onset of conduct disorder and to convey the alternative ways in which individual factors are defined and studied. At the same time, there remain several complexities that have direct implications for interpreting the findings, for understanding the disorder, and for identifying at-risk children for preventive interventions.

Relations Among Risk Factors. One complexity pertains to the *interrelations among the factors*. In general, although individual risk factors can be delineated, they tend to come in packages. Thus at a given point in time, several factors may be present, for example, low income, large family size, overcrowding, poor housing, poor parental supervision, parent criminality, and marital discord. The co-occurrence makes identifying the unique contribution of individual factors somewhat difficult.

Risk factors, if not present in a package at a given point in time, may accrue together. Over time, several risk factors may become interrelated because the presence of one factor can augment the accumulation of other risk factors. For example, early academic dysfunction can lead to truancy and dropping out of school; these factors may then further increase the risk for conduct disorder. The accumulation of risk factors means that the specific role of a given factor in the causal sequence leading to conduct disorder may be difficult to discern.

Apart from their co-occurrence, individual risk factors may interact with each other and with other variables (see Boyle & Offord, 1990). Interaction means that a given factor is influenced (e.g., attenuated or exacerbated in its effect) by another variable. As a simple example, large family size has been repeatedly shown to be a risk factor for conduct disorder. However, the importance of family size as a predictor is moderated by (i.e., interacts with) income. If family income and living accommodations are adequate, family size is less likely to be a risk factor. Family size exerts a greater influence on risk in lower-income homes, where overcrowding and other problems are present (West, 1982).

Age and Sex. Interactions of risk factors with age and sex warrant some comment in their own right. Both the specific factors and the strength of the associations between factors predicting the onset of dysfunction may vary at the point or stage in which they are assessed (e.g., infancy, early or middle childhood). For example, marital discord or separation appear to serve as risk factors when they occur early in the child's life (e.g., within the first 4 or 5 years) (Wadsworth, 1979). In addition, risk factors vary in the time when they can emerge. Some risk factors can be evident early in life and continue through childhood (e.g., poverty, poor living conditions); others emerge at specific points (e.g., school performance). This means that for a given age, factors used to identify children at risk and the weight accorded a given set of factors might vary.

Age enters into risk in yet another way. Outcomes at different time periods, such as early versus late onset of conduct disorder (e.g., between 10 and 13 years versus between 14 and 20 years), as well as continued conduct disorder (e.g., during ages 21 to 32 years) are predicted by different risk factors (Farrington & Hawkins, 1991). For example, poverty seems to serve as a risk factor for child-onset but not for adolescent-onset conduct disorder (Offord et al., 1991; Rutter, 1981). Thus specifying the age of the outcomes that are to be evaluated influences the specific factors to be used for early identification.

Risk factors also vary as a function of a child's sex. In some cases, both sexes may be influenced by a factor, although the strength of association may vary between the sexes. In other cases, the influence may be a risk factor for one sex but not for the other. For example, teacher ratings of aggression in the first grade predict delinquency years later for males but not for females (Tremblay et al., 1992). More generally, the profile of risk factors can vary markedly among males and females, as illustrated by work on the influence of genetic and environmental factors. In studies of adoptees, having an alcoholic biological relative, adverse home conditions in the adoptive home, and discontinuous mothering predicted conduct disorder in adolescent males (Cadoret & Cain, 1980, 1981). However, for female adolescents, having an antisocial or mentally retarded biological parent was the only predictor of conduct disorder. Environmental factors (i.e., home conditions and mothering practices) emerged as predictors only for males, suggesting their greater susceptibility to such influences. Other studies have suggested sex differences in vulnerability to environmental factors that may place the child at risk for conduct disorder (e.g., divorce or institutional care); however, many of these influences appear to be a matter of degree rather than an all-or-none phenomenon (Cloninger, Reich, & Guze, 1978; Wolkind & Rutter, 1973).

General Comments

The preceding comments convey salient complexities of risk factors in relation to the onset of conduct disorder. Two of the complexities embedded in the very notion of risk factor warrant reiteration. First, risk factors increase the likelihood of an outcome; they do not guarantee the outcome. The benefits and limitations of knowing that risk factors are present must be kept in mind. Even under very adverse conditions with multiple risk factors present, many individuals will adapt and not experience adverse outcomes (e.g., Richters & Martinez, 1993). Thus risk factors do not determine or invariably lead to a particular outcome.

Second, the risk factors do not tell us how a dysfunction comes about. Separate lines of research are required to focus on how these factors operate and combine, and why they may affect some youths but not others. Without this latter research, understanding is quite limited. Identifying what the risk factors are, how they interrelate, and the ways in which they operate are all important for developing methods to prevent the onset of disorder.

PROTECTIVE FACTORS

Obviously, not all individuals at risk for conduct disorder will evince later dysfunction. This can be assumed as a consequence of imperfections of assessment, including assessment of risk (i.e., the predictors), assessment of disorder (i.e., the criterion), and assessment of changes in the risk status on a particular factor over time. A conceptually interesting and potentially critical set of influences that may affect onset are referred to as *protective factors*. These factors refer to influences that may cancel or attenuate the influence of known risk factors and, in some way, increase resilience. As mentioned earlier, protective factors have been less well studied than risk factors, even though significant progress has been made within the last few years (see Cicchetti & Garmezy, 1993).

Salient Influences

Researchers have identified protective factors in two ways: by studying individuals known to be at risk due to the presence of several risk factors of the ilk discussed previously and by delineating subgroups of those who do versus those who do not later show conduct disorder. For example, in a longitudinal study from birth through young adulthood, youths were identified as at risk for delinquency based on a number of risk factors (Werner & Smith, 1992). Not all youths at risk became delinquent. Those youths who did not evince delinquency by adolescence were more likely to be first born, to be perceived by their mothers as affectionate, to show higher self-esteem and locus of control, and to have alternative caretakers in the family (rather than the parents) and a supportive same-sex role-model who played an important role in their development. Other factors that reduce or attenuate risk consist of above-average intelligence, competence in various skill areas, getting along with peers, and having friends (Rae Grant, Thomas, Offord, & Boyle, 1989). In many cases, protective factors seem to be the absence or inverse of a risk factor. Thus easy temperament, academic success, and good relations with parents reduce risk. One factor that emerges often is a good relationship with an emotionally responsive, caregiving adult, either a parent or a nonparent figure.

Identifying individual factors that serve a protective function may not convey either the type of more general influences or how they emerge and operate over the course of development. Among the many factors that emerge, three general categories are useful as a way to organize current findings (see Garmezy, 1985; Werner & Smith, 1992). The first is personal attributes of the individual. Beginning in infancy and unfolding throughout development, these include such factors as easy temperament, sociability, competencies at school, and high self-esteem. The second category seems to be family factors, including such characteristics as caretaking styles, education of the parents, and parent social competence. The third category consists of external supports, such as friendship and peer relations, and support from another significant adult. These are useful ways to identify main protective factors, but the categories no doubt distort how the factors operate. The reason is that these factors tend to be interdependent and reciprocal. For example, child attachment to the parent is important as a protective factor and probably reflects personal attributes of the child in combination with characteristics of the parent. The listing of protective factors in this static fashion ought not to distort their dynamic and reciprocal nature. In this sense, it is useful to conceptualize many of these factors as part of transactions between the child and the environment.

General Comments

Overall, much less is known about protective factors than is known about risk factors in relation to conduct disorder. In addition, the interpretation of these factors and the means through which they operate are not clear. Even so, protective factors are the focus of many preventive efforts designed to increase resilience of youths who are at risk (McCord & Tremblay, 1992). These preventive efforts, to be discussed further in a later chapter, focus on skills designed to protect against untoward influences that can lead to maladjustment. It may be that general competence-building can prevent conduct disorder. Alternatively, it may well be that the complexion of protective factors is as intricate as that of risk factors. That is, there may be several different factors that can protect or counteract risk factors; these may vary by child age, sex, and the influence of other protective factors. Evaluation of protective factors warrants much further work because fostering these factors represents a viable approach to preventing conduct disorder.

MECHANISMS AND PROCESSES LEADING TO CONDUCT DISORDER

Risk and protective factors provide initial leads regarding what is involved in the onset and continuation of conduct disorder. It is important to understand their limitations as well. We are interested in risk and protective factors in order to understand how the disorder unfolds, to prevent its onset, and to provide treatment when the disorder is evident. Identification of a risk factor does not necessarily provide in-depth understanding, even though this is a critical initial step. Understanding in this context refers to how the factor operates or the process through which it leads to deviant child behavior. For example, how does marital conflict or poor child supervision promote or lead to fighting, stealing, truancy, and setting fires? It is the process behind the risk factors that we wish to understand. Without understanding, our efforts to intervene can be misplaced. As an extreme illustration, we know that being a short, bald, male places one at risk for heart disease. It might be possible to intervene simply with one or more of these risks (e.g., by providing elevator shoes and a toupee). However, such interventions probably reflect a misunderstanding of why and how the factors placed individuals at risk.

Research has advanced in examining mechanisms or processes through which risk factors may operate. For example, neuropsychological impairment may place youths at risk for aggressive behavior, but how? A possible mechanism is that the neuropsychological impairment alters the infants' thresholds for reacting to the environment (i.e., producing a more difficult temperament). This, in turn, may alter the responses these infants evoke from others (e.g., producing a more negative parent reaction including harsh discipline). In this way, a sequence of processes and consequences that connect risk factors begins to elaborate how conduct disorder might unfold.

Separate lines of work can be identified to explain how characteristics that differentiate conduct and nonconduct disorder youths may operate to produce or contribute to the disorder. Consider briefly three broad approaches that identify possible underpinnings of conduct disorder and how they operate. *Psychobiological differences* have been proposed to underlie conduct disorder either through a direct influence or indirectly through increasing vulnerabilities to other influences. Brain differences have been proposed to explain the behavior of aggressive youths (Quay, 1993). Evidence suggests that behavioral inhibition and reward systems of the brain influence responding as well as failure to learn from the environment in critical ways (e.g., failure to respond well to punishing experiences that inhibit responding). A deficit in inhibition and an excess in reward-controlled aggressive behavior (e.g., predatory aggression) have been proposed as particularly important. Tests of these hypotheses involve primarily evaluation of neurotransmitters and biochemical activity of the brain (e.g., noradrenalin, serotonin) that reflect impaired inhibition and activation and the relation of this impairment to other measures of aggression (e.g., parent and teacher ratings or interviews) (see Lahey, Hart, Pliszka, Applegate, & McBurnett, 1993; Quay, 1993; Rogeness, Javors, & Pliszka, 1992). Supportive evidence has been found in relation to diagnosis of conduct disorder versus other diagnostic groups as well as in studies showing that biochemical differences (e.g., in a serotonin metabolite) in children predict levels of aggression up to 2 years later (e.g., Kruesi et al., 1990, 1992).

The focus on neurological systems is only one line of biological work focusing on mechanisms. Biochemical underpinnings of aggression have been investigated for some time (see Rutter & Giller, 1983). For example, plasma testosterone is elevated among violent delinquents compared to "normal" controls; it is positively correlated with low frustration tolerance and self-reports of verbal and physical aggression among nonclinic samples, particularly in response to provocation and threat (Mattsson et al., 1980; Olweus, Mattsson, Schalling, & Low, 1980). Perhaps testosterone plays a central role in aggression rather than in conduct disorder more generally, because testosterone was not found to be related to antisocial behaviors such as theft, truancy, and property destruction. Yet the relation of testosterone to aggression is not always found. Consequently, fundamental questions and the possible role of key moderators influencing this relation remain to be addressed (see Constatino et al., 1993).

Several mechanisms have been proposed that focus on interpersonal factors leading to the emergence of conduct disorder. Prominent among such factors is the *role of child-parent interaction* in which aggressive behavior is fostered in the child (Patterson et al., 1992). A social interactional view has been proposed in which a child's interpersonal style is learned within the family and extends to others (e.g., peers, teachers) outside the family. The pattern of family interaction includes inept discipline practices and coercive exchanges leading to escalation of child aggression. Research has shown that parents of aggressive children inadvertently promote this antisocial behavior by pervasively poor parenting skills (see Patterson et al., 1992). Compared to parents of nonclinic children, these parents punish inconsistently but quite frequently and ineffectively, they attend to and reward inappropriate child behavior, and they reinforce extremely coercive and aversive child behaviors (e.g., yelling and screaming).

The use of harsh punishment in the home can be seen to be more than merely a correlated antecedent of aggressive child behavior. Administration of corporal punishment is likely to have side effects that include aggression toward others. Hence it is no surprise that children punished severely are more likely to become aggressive. In any case, the consequences of early interactional patterns appear to spread to other areas. By middle childhood, the child's deviant behaviors lead to rejection of the child by nondeviant peers and to academic failure at school. These latter features in turn lead, in late childhood and early adolescence, to interactions with deviant peers and then to conduct disorder and delinquency. The proposed sequence has support from longitudinal studies; it conveys how deviant behavior unfolds and possibly comes under the influence of several different factors at different points over the course of development (Patterson et al., 1991, 1992).

Other research on the mechanisms or processes leading to conduct disorder integrates findings on social information processing (Crick & Dodge, 1994; Dodge, 1985). A significant component of this includes an *attributional bias* among aggressive children and adolescents. Aggressive youths tend to view ambiguous situations (i.e., those in which the intentions of others are unclear) as hostile. The attribution of hostility to others helps to precipitate aggressive acts that are merely retaliatory from the standpoint of the aggressive child. These acts, however, do not seem justified in the views of the child's peers. Peer rejection appears to follow aggressive behavior. The reactions of the peers, and their dislike of, and isolation from, the aggressive child provide additional cues to the aggressive child that the environment is hostile. Thus a vicious circle of aggressive behavior and untoward peer reactions can be sustained.

The focus on characteristics such as child-rearing practices or attributions helps to elaborate the ways in which correlates and risk factors might operate. In each case, a key construct is a point of departure to identify interrelations among current and subsequent facets of conduct disorder. The point-of-departure notion is critical because understanding the mechanisms of a particular influence leads to hypotheses and to tests of how other influences might operate. In this discussion, how biological and social interactional influences might operate were mentioned. Understanding one can inform the other. For example, harsh punishment can increase risk for conduct disorder. This may operate through social learning (e.g., modeling of aggressive behavior, displacement of aggression) as well as through physiological processes within the individual (e.g., hormone and neurotransmitter response to stress) that may increase the likelihood of problem behavior or vulnerability to other influences (Lewis, 1992). The task of research is to identify how specific influences operate and how they relate to, affect, and interact with other influences.

CONDUCT DISORDER
OVER THE LIFE SPAN

We have focused on risk factors for the onset of conduct disorder. There are broader questions in which we are interested, including what happens to youths with conduct disorder as they enter adulthood and, more generally, what are the characteristics and patterns of conduct disorder over the entire life span from birth through adulthood.

Continuation of Conduct Disorder in Adulthood

Considerable research has examined the outcome of conduct disorder identified in childhood, so let us begin here. Longitudinal studies have consistently shown that conduct disorder identified in childhood or adolescence predicts a continued course of social dysfunction, problematic behavior, and poor school and occupational adjustment (Farrington, 1991). One of the most dramatic illustrations of the long-term prognosis of clinically referred children was the classic study by Robins (1966) who evaluated their status 30 years later. The results demon-

TABLE 3.1 Long-Term Prognosis of Youths Identified as Conduct Disorder: Overview of Major Characteristics Likely to Be Evident in Adulthood

---

Characteristics in Adulthood

---

1. **Psychiatric Status:** Greater psychiatric impairment, including antisocial personality, alcohol and drug abuse, and isolated symptoms (e.g., anxiety, somatic complaints); also, greater history of psychiatric hospitalization.

2. **Criminal Behavior:** Higher rates of driving while intoxicated, criminal behavior, arrests, convictions, and periods of time spent in jail; greater seriousness of the criminal acts.

3. **Occupational Adjustment:** Less likely to be employed; shorter history of employment, lower status jobs, more frequent job changes, lower wages, and more frequently depending on financial assistance (welfare); serving less frequently and performing less well in the armed services.

4. **Educational Attainment:** Higher rates of dropping out of school, lower levels of educational attainment among those who remain in school.

5. **Marital Status:** Higher rates of divorce, remarriage, and separation.

6. **Social Participation:** Less contact with relatives, friends, and neighbors; little participation in organizations such as church.

7. **Physical Health:** Higher mortality rates; higher rates of hospitalization for physical (as well as psychiatric) problems.

NOTE: These characteristics are based on comparisons of clinically referred children identified for conduct disorder relative to control clinical referrals or to normal controls or from comparisons of delinquent and nondelinquent youths (for further discussion, see Farrington, 1991; Loeber, 1990; Robins, 1978; Rutter & Giller, 1983).

strated that antisocial child behavior predicted multiple problems in adulthood. Youths who had been referred for their conduct disorder, compared to youths with other clinical problems or with matched "normal" (i.e., nonreferred) controls, as adults were found to suffer psychiatric symptoms, criminal behavior, physical health dysfunctions, and poor social adjustment. Several studies are now available that attest to the breadth of dysfunction of conduct disorder children or adolescents as they mature into adulthood. These studies show that early signs of conduct disorder, whether identified from parent, teacher, or peer ratings, predict later conduct disorder up to 10, 20, and even 30 years later (see Farrington, 1991). Table 3.1 highlights the characteristics that conduct disorder youths are likely to show when they become adults.

Even though conduct disorder in childhood portends a number of other significant problems in adulthood, not all antisocial children suffer impairment as adults. Among several different samples, Robins (1978) found that fewer than 50% of the most severely antisocial children become antisocial adults. Some evidence suggests that there are important sex differences in continuation of conduct disorder into adulthood (Quinton, Rutter, & Gulliver, 1990). Boys are much more likely to continue conduct disorder into adulthood (in the form of antisocial personality disorder). In contrast, girls are likely to shift into more internalizing types of disorders (e.g., depression, anxiety) in adulthood.

Overall, sampling across males and females, less than half of the children continue conduct disorder into adulthood. If diverse diagnoses are considered, rather than continuation of conduct disorder alone, the picture of impairment in adulthood is much worse. Among children referred for conduct disorder, 84% received a diagnosis of psychiatric disorder as adults (Robins, 1966). Although these diagnoses vary in degree of impairment (e.g., psychoses, neuroses), the data suggest that the majority of children with conduct disorder will suffer from a significant degree of impairment. Thus the prognosis is relatively poor considering only subsequent psychiatric impairment. Such impairment obviously is likely to correlate with performance in other spheres (see Table 3.1).

As noted above, not all conduct disorder youths continue this pattern of dysfunction as they become adults. As with the onset of conduct disorder, several risk factors have been identified for the continuation of these behaviors. Major factors that influence whether conduct disorder is likely to continue into adulthood are summarized in Table 3.2. The factors are only highlighted here in part because they resemble those factors already discussed in relation to the onset of conduct disorder. As in the earlier discussion, the complexity of prognosticators is not fully conveyed by merely enumerating individual risk factors. For example, the risk for a long-term conduct disorder in adulthood is increased when the father has a history of conduct disorder and alcoholism (as noted in Table 3.2). This risk is increased when both the father and mother have been antisocial and alcoholic. However, when the mother alone shows these characteristics, the child is not at increased risk for antisocial personality (Robins, 1966). Thus within a given variable, and among alternative variables, the relationships may be relatively complex. Also, as noted before, it is likely that some risk factors are more important than others. In this regard, for example, early signs of conduct disorder are among the more salient predictors (Loeber &

TABLE 3.2 Characteristics That Predict Continued Conduct Disorder in Adulthood

---

Characteristic and Specific Pattern

---

1. **Age of Onset:** Earlier onset (e.g., before age 10 or 12) of conduct disorder. Early onset also is related to rate and seriousness of later conduct disorder.

2. **Breadth of Deviance:** A greater number of different types of antisocial behaviors; a greater variety of situations in which antisocial behavior is manifest (e.g., at home, school); a greater range of persons or organizations against which such behaviors are expressed.

3. **Frequency of Antisocial Behavior:** A greater number of different antisocial episodes (independent of whether they include a number of different behaviors).

4. **Seriousness of the Behavior:** Relatively serious antisocial behavior in childhood, especially if the behavior could be grounds for adjudication.

5. **Type of Symptoms:** Specific antisocial behaviors—lying, impulsiveness, truancy, running away, theft, and staying out late. Also, they may show nonantisocial symptoms of slovenliness and enuresis (after age 6).

6. **Parent Characteristics:** Parent psychopathology, particularly of conduct disorder; paternal record of arrests, unemployment, and alcoholism; poor parental supervision of child; overly strict, lax, or inconsistent discipline.

7. **Family:** A greater number from homes with marital discord and larger family size.

NOTE: These characteristics are based on comparisons of clinically referred children identified for conduct disorder relative to control clinic referrals or normal controls or from comparisons of delinquent and nondelinquent youths (for further discussion, see Farrington, 1991; Henggeler, 1989; Kazdin, 1985; Patterson et al., 1992).

Dishion, 1983; Rutter & Giller, 1983). Yet the number of risk factors also appears to be critical, so that the accumulation of a larger number greatly increases risk.

A Life Span Perspective

That conduct disorder continues into adulthood for many youths conveys that it is a serious and life-long dysfunction. A goal of theory and research is to understand the signs, manifestations, and course of conduct disorder over the entire life span from birth through adulthood. The emphasis on school-age youths in the study of conduct disorder and delinquency has provided considerable evidence about dysfunction within this age range. Also, many of the symptoms that define Conduct Disorder as a diagnosis are likely to be evident in late childhood and early adolescence (e.g., at 7 to 12 years of age). We wish to understand conduct disorder over the entire course of development. When does conduct disorder begin, what does "it" look like in the repertoires of individuals over the course of development, and how does it unfold?

Obviously, characteristics of conduct disorder are likely to look very different for a given individual over the entire course of development. A useful notion to handle these differences is referred to as *heterotypic continuity* (see Kagan, 1969). The concept denotes that specific manifestations of behavior such as conduct disorder are likely to change over the course of development. However, there may be a continuity in the inferred trait or characteristic that underlies these specific behaviors. For example, children with conduct problems may be mildly stubborn and break other children's toys and "borrow" (i.e., take) things that belong to their friends. However, stubbornness, breaking things, and taking things among young children (e.g., 3 to 4 years) may not predict these same behaviors 10 years later. Nonetheless, these early behaviors may predict behaviors that are conceptually related or that belong to the same general class of behaviors (e.g., stealing from stores and confronting strangers with a weapon).

Problem behavior theory, mentioned earlier, is one way of considering a consistent underlying characteristic to unify different types of deviant behavior over the course of development (Jessor et al., 1991). The theory postulates that multiple deviant behaviors may go together (e.g., drug use, early sexual activity) and that these are unified insofar as they are alternative ways of serving specific functions (e.g., obtaining independence from parents). Another way to refer to this view in relation to the present discussion is to consider the possibility that there is a general deviance syndrome consisting of a variety of deviant (conduct problem) behaviors (McGee & Newcomb, 1992). In fact, evidence suggests that several characteristics go together as a package (e.g., alcohol and drug use, criminal behavior, sexual involvement, lack of social conformity) and that a package of deviant behaviors, not necessarily the same behaviors, continues over the course of development (childhood, adolescence, and early adulthood). From the standpoint of a general deviance syndrome, it might be meaningful to identify youths on the basis of this underlying pattern. The overall pattern may be a meaningful way to consider the continuities over the course of development. In addition, there may be subpatterns that can be reliably detected.

Much of research designed to illuminate conduct disorder focuses on specific paths and transitions of development. In this work, the task is to identify the characteristics and signs of dysfunction over the stream of development and to identify how and when manifestations shift (see Peters, McMahon, & Quinsey, 1992). Longitudinal studies have been conducted in which youths are studied over a period of years, ranging from only a few years to the entire developmental period from birth through adolescence and young adulthood (e.g., Farrington, 1991; Werner & Smith, 1992). In the latter type of research, youths are sampled at multiple points (e.g., every few years) so that one can identify early predictors of later behavior, for example, what adolescents who are delinquent at some point "looked like" when they were infants and younger children.

Possible paths or trajectories of the development of conduct disorder can emerge from this work. The conclusions from such work have already been implied in many of our prior discussions. For example, child- and adolescent-onset conduct disorder are based on research suggesting that there are two patterns and that they have different antecedents, characteristics, and outcomes. For conduct disorder more generally, it is likely that there are multiple paths. For example, stubbornness, noncompliance, and defiance early in childhood tend to precede conduct disorder (e.g., Lahey et al., 1992; Loeber, Keenan et al., 1993). In terms of diagnoses, Oppositional Defiant Disorder characterizes the former, and for many youths that diagnosis precedes a Conduct Disorder diagnosis. Yet many youths with Oppositional Defiant Disorder never develop Conduct Disorder and many Conduct Disorder youths do not show an earlier history of Oppositional Defiant Disorder. Even so, evidence points to considerable stability over the course of development and progressions of conduct problem behavior. Early behaviors (e.g., disobedience, tantrums) are likely to provide a preview of other behaviors (e.g., physical aggression), and in turn these begin to have broad ramifications for behaviors in many other domains (e.g., peers relation, school performance) (e.g., Patterson, 1992). Work has begun to chart these progressions over the entire life span (see Peters et al., 1992).

SUMMARY AND CONCLUSIONS

Several factors have been identified that place a child at risk for conduct disorder. Early signs of troublesome or obstreperous behavior at home or at school are salient predictors. In addition, a variety of parent and family characteristics have been identified as risk factors, such as genetic factors, criminality, conduct disorder and alcoholism in the parents, marital discord, and harsh and inconsistent discipline practices. Although less well researched, a number of protective factors have also been identified. These provide some leads regarding how to aid populations at risk. Studies of the mechanisms or means through which risk factors operate elaborate the processes leading to conduct disorder. Such work, along with understanding protective factors, provides leads regarding how to intervene. Among the challenges to this work are identifying how various influences operate alone and in combination; how these influences operate at different points in development; and how the influences operate among youths who differ in sex, ethnicity, and perhaps subtype of conduct problems.

The study of risk factors, onset and clinical course has revealed the considerable stability and continuity of conduct disorder, not only from childhood through adolescence and adulthood, but also in transgenerational continuity. Adoption studies and studies of dysfunction in parents and grandparents of conduct disorder youths have helped to establish the continuity across generations. Although the precise bases for this continuity (e.g., the extent to which particular gene-action models apply, the influence of socioenvironmental factors) are not well understood, the fact that conduct disorder generally has a continuous course is noteworthy. The stability and continuity of conduct disorder mean that interventions designed to ameliorate these behaviors are quite important. The next chapters review and evaluate treatment and preventive techniques.

4

CURRENT TREATMENTS

Treatment refers to systematic efforts to reduce, alleviate, or eliminate a problem. In light of what has been discussed so far, the task of treatments for conduct disorder is enormous. Conduct disorder youths are likely to experience a broad range of dysfunctions (e.g., conduct problem symptoms, impairment in social and academic behavior). Moreover, their parents and families may also show problems that affect and are affected by the children (e.g., parent psychopathology, marital discord). A variety of interventions have been applied with conduct disorder youths, including psychotherapy; medication; home-, school-, and community-based programs; residential and hospital treatment; and social services (for reviews, see Brandt & Zlotnick, 1988; Dumas, 1989; Kazdin, 1985; U.S. Congress, 1991). A small number of treatments have been shown to reduce conduct disorder in children and adolescents. This chapter highlights the most promising treatment approaches and conveys what has and has not been accomplished to date.

IDENTIFYING EFFECTIVE TREATMENTS

The chapter focuses on psychological interventions or types of psychotherapy, broadly conceived, because they represent the bulk of research and the most promising approaches. Table 4.1 highlights major classes of psychotherapy and their therapeutic focus. The classes are a useful way to consider broad differences among available treatments. Yet within a given type of treatment several variations can be identified. For example, individual psychotherapy consists of psychodynamic therapy, nondirective therapy, play therapy, and other types. Similarly, behavior therapy can include a range of techniques, such as social skills training, contingency management, and token economies. At the level of specific techniques (rather than the more generic classes

TABLE 4.1 Therapeutic Focus and Processes of Major Classes of Treatment for Antisocial Behavior

Types of Treatment	Focus	Key Processes
Child-Focused Treatments		
Individual Psychotherapy	Focus on intrapsychic bases of antisocial behavior, especially conflicts and psychological processes that were adversely affected over the course of development.	Relationship with the therapists is the primary medium through which change is achieved. Treatment provides a corrective emotional experience by providing insight and exploring new ways of behaving.
Group Psychotherapy	Processes of individual therapy, as noted above. Additional processes are reassurance, feedback, and vicarious gains by peers. Group processes such as cohesion, leadership also serve as the focus.	Relationship with the therapist and peers as part of the group. Group processes emerge to provide children with experiences and feelings of others and opportunities to test their own views and behaviors.
Behavior Therapy	Problematic behaviors presenting as target symptoms or behaviors designed to controvert these symptoms (e.g., prosocial behaviors) are trained directly.	Learning of new behaviors through direct training, via modeling, reinforcement, practice and role playing. Training in the situations (e.g., at home, in the community) where the problematic behaviors occur.
Cognitively Based Treatment	Cognitive processes and interpersonal cognitive problem-solving skills that underlie social behavior.	Teach problem-solving skills to children by engaging in a step-by-step approach to interpersonal situations. Use of modeling, practice, rehearsal, and role play to develop skills. Development of an internal dialogue or private speech that utilizes the processes of identifying prosocial solutions to problems.
Pharmacotherapy	Designed to affect the biological substrates of behavior, especially in light of laboratory-based findings on neurohumors, biological cycles, and other physiological correlates of aggressive and emotional behavior.	Administration of psychotropic agents to control antisocial behavior. Lithium carbonate and haloperidol have been used because of their antiaggressive effects.

TABLE 4.1 Continued

Types of Treatment	*Focus*	*Key Processes*
Residential Treatments	Means of administering other techniques in day treatment or residential setting. Foci of other techniques apply.	Processes of other techniques apply. Also, separation of the child from parents or removal from the home may help reduce untoward processes or crises that contribute to the clinical problem.

Family-Focused Treatments

Family Therapy	Family as a functioning system serves as focus rather than the identified patient. Interpersonal relationships, organization, roles, and dynamics of the family.	Communication, relationships, and structure within the family and processes such as autonomy, problem solving, and negotiation.
Parent Management Training	Interactions in the home, especially those involving coercive exchanges.	Direct training of parents to develop prosocial behavior in their children. Explicit use of social learning techniques to influence the child.

Community-Based Treatments

Community-Wide Interventions	Focus on activities and community programs to foster competence and peer relations.	Develop prosocial behavior and connections with peers. Activities are seen to promote prosocial behavior and to be incompatible with antisocial behavior.

of treatment), the number of procedures would be large. In fact, well over 200 different therapy techniques can be identified that are in use in clinical practice (Kazdin, 1988). All of the treatments are well intentioned, most are reasonable, and several appeal to common sense (e.g., conduct problem youths are angry and need to talk about their feelings). It is a fact that most treatments have no evidence in their behalf. Thus, with a myriad of treatments available, the key question is how to identify which of the treatments are promising.

To sort through such a large number of treatments, it is useful to consider criteria that might be invoked to identify promising treatments. In our own work, we have relied on several criteria to identify

TABLE 4.2 Criteria for Identifying Promising Treatments

---

1. **Conceptualization:** Theoretical statement relating the mechanism(s) (e.g., intrapsychic, intrafamilial) to clinical dysfunction.

2. **Basic Research:** Evidence showing that the mechanism can be assessed and relates to dysfunction, independently of treatment outcome studies.

3. **Preliminary Outcome Evidence:** Evidence in analogue or clinical research showing that the approach leads to change on clinically relevant measures.

4. **Process-Outcome Connection:** Evidence in outcome studies showing a relationship between the change in processes alleged to be operative and clinical outcome.

---

and to select those that are promising (see Table 4.2). The initial criterion is that the treatment should have some theoretical rationale that specifies how the dysfunction, in this case conduct disorder, comes about and how treatment redresses the dysfunction. The mechanisms leading to conduct disorder and leading to therapeutic change are required for this initial criterion.

The second criterion considers whether there is any basic research to support the conceptualization. Basic research in this context refers to studies that examine conduct problems and the factors that lead to the onset, maintenance, exacerbation, amelioration, or attenuation of these problems. An example would be studies of the family that demonstrate specific interaction patterns among parents and children that exacerbate aggression within the home. Such research would advance considerably a conceptual view that posits the significance of these patterns and provides a conceptual basis for developing treatments that are aimed at these interaction patterns.

The third criterion is whether there is any outcome evidence that the treatment can produce change of any kind. Obviously, randomized clinical trials are preferred. However, because most treatments in use with children and adolescents have not been tested in controlled studies, it is useful to be lenient when invoking this criterion. If a technique has any data, controlled or otherwise, that suggest the technique can lead to change, this type of information would separate that treatment from the masses of others for which no data are available.

Finally, evidence showing that critical processes change in treatment and that these processes relate to outcome would indicate that the treatment is very promising indeed. For example, treatment may propose that changes in cognitions are required to change conduct problems. A treatment study showing that changes in these processes occur and correlate with changes in treatment outcome (e.g., deviant behavior at school) would considerably advance the case for that treatment. This is a rather stringent criterion and hence might be useful to bear in mind rather than to invoke stringently.

No single treatment among those available adequately traverses these criteria. Yet a number of promising treatments have been identified for conduct disorder. Treatment approaches that most closely approximate the criteria convey considerable promise and are illustrated here. These include cognitive problem-solving skills training, parent management training, functional family therapy, and multisystemic therapy.[1]

HIGHLY PROMISING APPROACHES

Cognitive Problem-Solving Skills Training

Background and Underlying Rationale. Cognitive processes refer to broad classes of constructs that pertain to how an individual perceives, codes, and experiences the world. Individuals who engage in conduct disorder behaviors, particularly aggression, have been found to show distortions and deficiencies in various cognitive processes. These deficiencies are not merely reflections of intellectual functioning. Although selected processes (e.g., recall, information processing) are related to intellectual functioning, their impact has been delineated separately and has been shown to contribute to behavioral adjustment and social behavior.

A variety of cognitive processes have been studied, including the abilities to generate alternative solutions to interpersonal problems (e.g., different ways of handling social situations); to identify the means to obtain particular ends (e.g., making friends) or consequences of actions (e.g., what could happen after a particular behavior); to make attributions to others of the motivation of their actions; to perceive how others feel; and to formulate expectations of the effects of one's own actions (see Shirk, 1988; Spivack & Shure, 1982). Deficits and distortion among these processes relate to teacher ratings of disruptive behavior, peer evaluations, and direct assessment of overt behavior (e.g., Lochman & Dodge, 1994; Rubin, Bream, & Rose-Krasnor, 1991).

As an illustration, aggression is not merely triggered by environmental events, but rather through the way in which these events are perceived and processed. The processing refers to the child's appraisals of the situation, the anticipated reactions of others, and the child's self-statements in response to particular events. For example, attribution of intent to others represents a salient cognitive disposition critically important to understanding aggressive behavior. As mentioned previously, aggressive youths tend to attribute hostile intent to others, especially in social situations in which the cues of actual intent are often ambiguous (see Crick & Dodge, 1994). Understandably, when situations are initially perceived as hostile, youths are more likely to react aggressively.

Although many studies have shown conduct disorder youths experience various cognitive distortions and deficiencies, fundamental questions remain to be resolved. Among these questions are the specificity of cognitive deficits among diagnostic groups and youth of different ages, whether some of the processes are more central than others, and how these processes unfold developmentally. Nevertheless, research on cognitive processes among aggressive children has served as a heuristic base for conceptualizing treatment and for developing specific treatment strategies.

Characteristics of Treatment. Problem-solving skills training (PSST) consists of developing interpersonal cognitive problem-solving skills. Although many variations of PSST have been applied to conduct problem children, several characteristics usually are shared. First, the emphasis is on *how* children approach situations. Although it is obviously important that children ultimately select appropriate means of behaving in everyday life, the primary focus is on the thought *processes* rather than the *outcome* or specific behavioral acts that result. Second, children are taught to engage in a step-by-step approach to solve interpersonal problems. They make statements to themselves that direct attention to certain aspects of the problem or tasks that lead to effective solutions. Third, treatment uses structured tasks involving games, academic activities, and stories. Over the course of treatment, the cognitive problem-solving skills are increasingly applied to real-life situations. Fourth, therapists usually play an active role in treatment. They model the cognitive processes by making verbal self-statements, apply the sequence of statements to particular problems, provide cues to prompt the use of the skills, and deliver feedback and praise to develop correct use of the skills. Finally, treatment usually combines several different procedures, including modeling and practice, role-playing, and reinforcement and mild punishment (loss of points or tokens).

Overview of the Evidence. Several outcome studies have been completed with impulsive, aggressive, and conduct disorder children and adolescents (for reviews, see Baer & Nietzel, 1991; Durlak, Fuhrman, & Lampman, 1991). The findings in many of these studies have indicated that cognitively based treatment has led to significant reductions in aggressive and antisocial behavior at home, at school, and in the community and that these gains are evident up to 1 year later. Many early studies in the field (e.g., 1970s and 1980s) focused on impulsive children and nonpatient samples. Since that time, several studies have shown treatment effects with clinically referred youths (see Kazdin, 1993; Kendall, 1991; Pepler & Rubin, 1991). Some evidence suggests that older children profit more from treatment than younger children, perhaps due to their cognitive development (Durlak et al., 1991). However, the basis for differential responsiveness to treatment as a function of age or severity of symptoms has not been well tested. Conduct disorder children from families with high levels of impairment (parent psychopathology, stress, and family dysfunction) respond less well to treatment than youths from families with less impairment (Kazdin, in press). Yet whether these factors are specific to problem-solving skills training or whether they influence the effectiveness of all treatments for conduct disorder youth has yet to be studied.

Overall Evaluation. There are features of PSST that make it an extremely promising approach. Perhaps most importantly, several controlled outcome studies with clinic samples have shown that cognitively based treatment leads to therapeutic change. Second, basic research in developmental psychology continues to elaborate the relation of maladaptive cognitive processes among children and adolescents and conduct problems that serve as underpinnings of treatment. Third, and on a more practical level, many variations of treatment are available in manual form (e.g., Finch, Nelson, & Ott, 1993; Shure, 1992). Consequently, the treatment can be evaluated in research and explored further in clinical practice.

Fundamental questions about treatment remain. To begin, the role of cognitive processes in clinical dysfunction and treatment warrant further evaluation. Evidence is not entirely clear showing that a specific pattern of cognitive processes characterizes youths with conduct problems rather than adjustment problems more generally. Also, although evidence has shown that cognitive processes change with treatment, evidence has not established that change in these processes is correlated with improvements in treatment outcome. This leaves unclear the bases for therapeutic change.

Also, developmental constructs, characteristics of children and their families, and parameters of treatment generally have not been explored in relation to treatment outcome. Finally, reliable changes have been achieved with treatment but the magnitude of change raises questions. Many youths improve but remain outside of the range of normative functioning relative to same age and sex peers (e.g., Kazdin, Bass, Siegel, & Thomas, 1989; Kazdin, Siegel, & Bass, 1992). Clearly, central questions about treatment and its effects remain to be resolved. Even so, PSST is highly promising because treatment effects have been replicated in several controlled studies with conduct disorder youth.

Parent Management Training

Background and Underlying Rationale. Parent management training (PMT) refers to procedures in which parents are trained to alter their child's behavior in the home. The parents meet with a therapist or trainer who teaches them to use specific procedures to alter interactions with their child, to promote prosocial behavior, and to decrease deviant behavior. Training is based on the general view that conduct problem behavior is inadvertently developed and sustained in the home by maladaptive parent-child interactions. There are multiple facets of parent-child interaction that promote aggressive and antisocial behavior. These patterns include directly reinforcing deviant behavior, frequently and ineffectively using commands and harsh punishment, and failing to attend to appropriate behavior (Patterson, 1982; Patterson et al., 1992).

It would be misleading to imply that the parent generates and is solely responsible for the child-parent sequences of interactions. Influences are bidirectional, so that the child influences the parent as well (see Bell & Harper, 1977; Lytton, 1990). In some cases, the children appear to engage in deviant behavior to help prompt the interaction sequences. For example, when parents behave inconsistently and unpredictably (e.g., not attending to the child in the usual ways), the child may engage in some deviant behavior (e.g., whining, throwing some object). The effect is to cause the parent to respond in more predictable ways (see Wahler & Dumas, 1986). Essentially, inconsistent and unpredictable parent behavior is an aversive condition for the child; the child's deviant behavior is negatively reinforced by terminating this condition. However, the result is also to increase parent punishment of the child.

Among the many interaction patterns, those involving coercion have received the greatest attention. *Coercion* refers to deviant behavior on the part of one person (e.g., the child) that is rewarded by another person (e.g., the parent). Aggressive children are inadvertently rewarded for their aggressive interactions and their escalation of coercive behaviors. The critical role of parent-child discipline practices in child antisocial behavior is not merely a plausible conceptual model. Support has evolved systematically from correlational data relating specific discipline practices to antisocial behavior and from experimental manipulations showing that directly altering these practices reduces antisocial child behavior (see Dishion, Patterson, & Kavanagh, 1992).

The general purpose of PMT is to alter the pattern of interchanges between parent and child so that prosocial rather than coercive behavior is directly reinforced and supported within the family. This requires developing several different parenting behaviors such as establishing the rules for the child to follow, providing positive reinforcement for appropriate behavior, delivering mild forms of punishment to suppress behavior, negotiating compromises, and other procedures. The inept discipline practices and coercive exchanges have direct implications for intervention.

Characteristics of Treatment. Although many variations of PMT exist, several common characteristics can be identified. First, treatment is conducted primarily with the parent(s) who implement several procedures in the home. The parents meet with a therapist who teaches them to use specific procedures to alter interactions with their child, to promote prosocial behavior and to decrease deviant behavior. There usually is little or no direct intervention of the therapist with the child. Second, parents are trained to identify, define, and observe problem behaviors in new ways. Careful specification of the problem is essential for the delivery of reinforcing or punishing consequences and for evaluating whether the program is achieving the desired goals. Third, the treatment sessions cover social learning principles and the procedures that follow from them. These include positive reinforcement (e.g., the use of social praise and tokens or points for prosocial behavior); mild punishment (e.g., use of time out from reinforcement, loss of privileges); negotiation; and contingency contracting. Fourth, the sessions provide opportunities for parents to see how the techniques are implemented, to practice using the techniques, and to review the behavior change programs in the home. The immediate goal of the program is to develop specific skills in the parents. As the parents become more proficient, the program can address the child's most severely problematic behaviors and encompass other problem areas (e.g., school behavior).

Overview of the Evidence. PMT is probably the best researched therapy technique for the treatment of conduct disorder youths. Scores of outcome studies have been completed with youths varying in age and degree of severity of dysfunction (e.g., oppositional, conduct disorder, delinquent youth) (see Kazdin, 1993; Miller & Prinz, 1990; Patterson, Dishion, & Chamberlain, 1993). The effectiveness of treatment has been evident in marked improvements in child behavior on a wide range of measures, including parent and teacher reports of deviant behavior, direct observation of behaviors at home and at school, and various institutional records (e.g., arrests). The effects of treatment have also been shown to bring the problematic behaviors of treated children within the normative levels of their peers who are functioning adequately. Follow-up assessment has shown that the gains are often maintained between for 1 and 3 years after treatment. Longer follow-ups are rarely used, although one program reported maintenance of gains 10 to 14 years later (Forehand & Long, 1988; Long, Forehand, Wierson, & Morgan, 1994).

The impact of PMT is relatively broad. The effects of treatment are evident for child behaviors that are not a direct focus of training. Also, siblings of children referred for treatment improve, even when they are not a direct focus of treatment. This is an important effect because siblings of conduct disorder youths are at risk for severe antisocial behavior. In addition, maternal psychopathology, particularly depression, has been shown to decrease systematically following PMT (see Kazdin, 1985). These changes suggest that PMT alters multiple aspects of dysfunctional families.

Several characteristics of the treatment contribute to outcome. Duration of treatment appears to influence outcome. Brief and time-limited treatments (e.g., less than 10 hours) are less likely to show benefits with clinical populations. More dramatic and durable effects have been achieved with protracted or time-unlimited programs extending up to

50 or 60 hours of treatment (see Kazdin, 1985). Second, specific training components such as providing parents with in-depth knowledge of social learning principles and using time out from reinforcement in the home enhance treatment effects. Third, some evidence suggests that therapist training and skill are associated with the magnitude and durability of therapeutic changes, although this has yet to be carefully tested. Fourth, families characterized by many risk factors associated with childhood dysfunction (e.g., socioeconomic disadvantage, marital discord, parent psychopathology, poor social support) tend to show fewer gains in treatment and to maintain the gains less well than families without these risk factors (e.g., Dadds & McHugh, 1992; Dumas & Wahler, 1983; Webster-Stratton, 1985). Some efforts to address parent and family dysfunction during PMT have led to improved effects of treatment outcome for the child (e.g., Dadds, Schwartz, & Sanders, 1987; Griest et al., 1982). However, much more work is needed on this issue.

Conceptual development of the processes underlying parent-child interactions and conduct disorder continues (e.g., Patterson et al., 1992). Also, recent research on processes in treatment represents a related and important advance. A series of studies on therapist parent interaction within PMT sessions has identified factors that contribute to parent resistance (e.g., parent saying, "I can't," "I won't"). The significance of this work is in showing that parent reactions in therapy relate to their discipline practices at home; that changes in resistance during therapy predict change in parent behavior; and that specific therapist ploys (e.g., reframing, confronting) can help overcome resistance or can contribute to it (Patterson & Chamberlain, 1994). This line of work advances our understanding of PMT greatly by relating in-session interactions of the therapist and parent to child functioning and treatment outcome.

Overall Evaluation. Perhaps the most important point to underscore is that probably no other technique for conduct disorder has been studied as often or as well in controlled trials as has PMT. The outcome data make PMT one of the most promising treatments. Along with outcome investigations, basic research has been conducted on family interaction patterns and influences outside of the home that may have impact on treatment outcome. This research is not only likely to contribute directly to improved treatment outcomes, but it may also enhance our understanding of the emergence of antisocial behavior.

A major advantage is the availability of treatment manuals and training materials for parents and professional therapists (e.g., Forehand & McMahon, 1981; Sanders & Dadds, 1993). Also noteworthy is the development of self-administered videotapes of treatment. In a programmatic series of studies with young (3- to 8-year-old) conduct problem children, Webster-Stratton and her colleagues have developed and evaluated videotaped materials that present PMT to parents in a self-administered (individual or group) format supplemented with discussion (e.g., Webster-Stratton, 1994; Webster-Stratton, Hollinsworth, & Kolpacoff, 1989). Controlled studies have shown clinically significant changes at posttreatment and follow-up assessments with variations of videotaped treatment. The potential for extension of PMT with readily available and empirically tested videotapes presents a unique feature in child treatment.

Several limitations of PMT can be identified as well. First, some families may not respond to treatment. PMT makes several demands on the parents, such as mastering the educational materials conveying the major principles underlying the program; systematically observing deviant child behavior; implementing specific procedures at home; attending weekly sessions; and responding to frequent telephone contacts made by the therapist. For some families, the demands may be too great to continue in treatment.

In addition, PMT has been applied primarily with parents of younger children and preadolescents and less often with adolescents. Although treatment has been effective with adolescents (Bank et al., 1991), evidence suggests that treatment is more effective with younger children (see Dishion & Patterson, 1992). Parents of adolescents may less readily change their discipline practices; they may also have higher rates of dropping out of treatment. It is important to note that few PMT programs have been developed specifically for adolescents. On balance, PMT is one of the most promising treatment modalities. No other intervention for conduct disorder has been investigated as thoroughly as PMT.

Functional Family Therapy

Background and Underlying Rationale. Functional family therapy (FFT) reflects an integrative approach to treatment that has relied on systems, behavioral, and cognitive views of dysfunction (Alexander, Holtzworth-Munroe, & Jameson, 1994; Alexander & Parsons, 1982).

Clinical problems are conceptualized from the standpoint of the functions they serve in the family as a system, as well as for individual family members. The assumption is made that problem behavior evident in the child is the only way some interpersonal functions (e.g., intimacy, distancing, support) can be met among family members. Maladaptive processes within the family are considered to preclude a more direct means of fulfilling these functions. The goal of treatment is to alter interaction and communication patterns in such a way as to foster more adaptive functioning. Treatment is also based on learning theory and focuses on specific stimuli and responses that can be used to produce change. Behavioral concepts and procedures identifying specific behaviors for change and reinforcing new adaptive ways of responding, and procedures empirically evaluating and monitoring change are included in this perspective. Cognitive processes refer to the attributions, attitudes, assumptions, expectations, and emotions of the family. Family members may begin treatment with attributions that focus on blaming others or themselves. New perspectives may be needed to help serve as the basis for developing new ways of behaving.

The underlying rationale emphasizes a family systems approach. Specific treatment strategies draw on findings that underlie PMT in relation to maladaptive and coercive parent-child interactions, discussed previously. FFT views interaction patterns from a broader systems view that focuses also on communication patterns and their meaning. As an illustration of the salient constructs, research underlying FFT has found that families of delinquents show higher rates of defensiveness in their communications, both in parent-child and parent-parent interactions, higher rates of blaming and negative attributions, and lower rates of mutual support compared to families of nondelinquents (see Alexander & Parsons, 1982). Improving these communication and support functions is a goal of treatment.

Characteristics of Treatment. FFT requires that the family see the clinical problem from the relational functions it serves within the family. The therapist points out interdependencies and contingencies between family members in their day-to-day functioning and with specific reference to the problem that has served as the basis for seeking treatment. Once the family sees alternative ways of viewing the problem, the incentive for interacting more constructively is increased.

The main goals of treatment are to increase reciprocity and positive reinforcement among family members, to establish clear communication, to help specify behaviors that family members desire from each other, to negotiate constructively, and to help identify solutions to interpersonal problems. In therapy, family members identify behaviors they would like others to perform. Responses are incorporated into a reinforcement system to be used in the home to promote adaptive behavior in exchange for privileges. However, the primary focus is within the treatment sessions in which family communication patterns are altered directly. During the sessions, the therapist provides social reinforcement (i.e., verbal and nonverbal praise) for communications that suggest solutions to problems, that clarify problems, or that offer feedback to other family members.

Overview of the Evidence. Relatively few outcome studies have evaluated FFT (see Alexander et al., 1994). However, the available studies have focused on difficult to treat populations (e.g., adjudicated delinquent adolescents, multiple offender delinquents) and have produced relatively clear effects. In controlled studies, comparisons reveal that FFT has led to greater change than either other treatment techniques (e.g., client-centered family groups, psychodynamically oriented family therapy) or various control conditions (e.g., group discussion and expression of feeling, nontreatment control groups). Treatment outcome is reflected in improved family communication and interactions and lower rates of referrals to and contacts with the courts. Moreover, gains have been evident up to 2½ years after treatment in several studies.

Research has examined processes in therapy to identify in-session behaviors of the therapist and how these influence responsiveness among family members (Alexander, Barton, Schiavo, & Parsons, 1976; Newberry, Alexander, & Turner, 1991). For example, providing support and structure as well as reframing (i.e., recasting the attributions and bases of a problem) can influence family member responsiveness and blaming of others. The relations among such variables are complex insofar as the impact of various types of statements (e.g., supportive) can vary as a function of the gender of the therapist and of the family member. Evidence of change in the processes proposed to be critical to FFT (e.g., improved communication in treatment, more spontaneous discussion) supports the conceptual view of treatment. For present purposes, the critical point is that processes of treatment contributing to outcome are being pursued in research.

Overall Evaluation. Several noteworthy points can be made about FFT. First, the outcome studies indicate that FFT can alter conduct problems among delinquent youth. Several studies have produced consistent effects. Second, the evaluation of processes within treatment that contribute to family member responsiveness within the sessions as well as outcome represents a line of work rarely seen among the treatment techniques for children and adolescents. Some of this process work has extended to laboratory (analogue) studies to examine more precisely how specific types of therapist statements (e.g., reframing) can reduce blaming among group members (e.g., Morris, Alexander, & Turner, 1991). Third, the treatment, as others mentioned previously, exists in manual form (Alexander & Parsons, 1982) and hence can be extended to treatment by others and be used to codify further advances in the treatment as they emerge from research. Further work extending FFT to children and to clinic populations would be of interest in addition to the current work with delinquent adolescents. Also, further work on child, parent, and family characteristics that moderate outcome would be a next logical step in the existing research program.

Multisystemic Therapy

Background and Underlying Rationale. Multisystemic therapy (MST) is a family-systems based approach to treatment (Henggeler & Borduin, 1990). Family approaches maintain that clinical problems of the child emerge within the context of the family; the focus is on treatment at that level. MST expands on that view by considering the family as one, albeit a very important, system. The child is embedded in a number of systems, including the family (immediate and extended family members), peers, schools, neighborhood, and so on. For example, within the context of the family, some tacit alliance between one parent and child may contribute to disagreement and conflict over discipline in relation to the child. Treatment may be required to address the alliance and sources of conflict in an effort to alter child behavior. Also, child functioning at school may involve limited and poor peer relations; treatment may address these areas as well. Finally, the systems approach entails a focus on the individual's own behavior insofar as it affects others. Individual treatment of the child or parents may be included in treatment.

Because multiple influences are entailed by the focus of the treatment, many different treatment techniques are used. Thus MST can be viewed as a package of interventions that are deployed with children and their families. Treatment procedures are used on an "as needed" basis directed toward addressing individual, family, and system issues that may contribute to problem behavior. The conceptual view focusing on multiple systems and their impact on the individual serves as a basis for selecting multiple and quite different treatment procedures.

Characteristics of Treatment. Central to MST is a family-based treatment approach. Several family therapy techniques (e.g., joining, reframing, enactment, paradox, and assigning specific tasks) are used to identify problems, increase communication, build cohesion, and alter how family members interact. Among the goals of treatment are to help the parents develop behaviors of the adolescent, to overcome marital difficulties that impede the parents' ability to function as parents, to eliminate negative interactions between parent and adolescent, and to develop or build cohesion and emotional warmth among family members.

MST draws on many other techniques as needed to address problems at the level of individual, family, and extrafamily. As prominent examples, PSST, PMT, and marital therapy are used in treatment to alter the response repertoire of the adolescent, parent-child interactions at home and marital communication, respectively. In some cases, treatment consists of helping the parents address a significant domain through practical advice and guidance (e.g., involving the adolescent in prosocial peer activities at school, restricting specific activities with a deviant peer group).

Although MST includes distinct techniques of other approaches, it is not a mere amalgamation of them. The focus of treatment is on interrelated systems and how they affect each other. Domains may be addressed in treatment (e.g., parent unemployment) because they raise issues for one or more systems (e.g., parent stress, increased alcohol consumption) that affect how the child is functioning (e.g., marital conflict, child discipline practices). Thus MST, although broad in treatment techniques, is not unbridled eclecticism.

Overview of the Evidence. A small number of outcome studies have evaluated MST with delinquent youths having arrest and incarceration histories, including violent crime (e.g., manslaughter, aggravated assault with intent to kill). Thus this was a group of extremely antisocial and aggressive youths. The results showed MST to be superior in reducing delinquency and emotional and behavioral problems and in improving family functioning in comparison to other procedures, including "usual services" provided to such youths (e.g., probation, court-ordered activities that are monitored, such as school attendance), individual counseling, and community-based eclectic treatment (e.g., Henggeler et al., 1986; Henggeler, Melton, & Smith, 1992). Follow-up studies up to 2, 4, and 5 years later with separate samples have shown that MST youths have lower arrest rates than youths who receive other services (see Henggeler, 1994).

Research has also shown that treatment affects critical processes proposed to contribute to deviant behavior (Mann, Borduin, Henggeler, & Blaske, 1990). Parents and teenage youths show reductions in coalitions (e.g., less verbal activity, conflict, and hostility) and increases in support; the parents show increases in verbal communication and decreases in conflict. Moreover, decreases in adolescent symptoms are positively correlated with increases in supportiveness and with decreases in conflict between the mother and father. This work provides an important link between theoretical underpinnings of treatment and outcome effects.

Overall Evaluation. Several outcome studies are available for MST and they are consistent in showing that treatment leads to change in adolescents and that the changes are sustained. A strength of the studies is that many of the youths who are treated are severely impaired (e.g., delinquent adolescents with a history of arrest). Another strength is the conceptualization of conduct problems at multiple levels—namely, as dysfunction in relation to the individual, family, and extrafamilial systems and the transactions among these. In fact, youths with conduct disorder experience dysfunction at multiple levels, including individual repertoires, family interactions, and extrafamilial systems (e.g., peers, schools, employment among later adolescents). Alternative treatment approaches invariably identify one of these as the main treatment focus. MST begins with the view that may different domains are likely to be relevant; these domains need to be evaluated and then addressed in treatment.

A difficulty of the approach is deciding which treatments to use in a given case among the many interventions encompassed by MST. Although guidelines are available to direct the therapist, they are somewhat general (e.g., focus on developing positive sequences of behaviors between systems such as parent and adolescent, evaluate the interventions during treatment so that changes can be made; see Henggeler,

1994). Providing interventions as needed is very difficult without a consistent way to assess what is needed, given inherent limits of decision making and perception, even among trained professionals. Yet there have been replications of MST beyond the original research program, indicating that treatment can be extended across settings.

On balance, MST is quite promising given the quality of evidence and consistency in the effects that have been produced. The promise stems from a conceptual approach that examines multiple domains (systems) and their contribution to dysfunction, evidence on processes in therapy and their relation to outcome, and the outcome studies themselves. Also, other literatures are relevant to MST because techniques such as PSST and PMT are incorporated into treatment within the multisystemic framework.

Other Treatments

The four treatments already discussed were selected for inclusion in light of criteria enumerated earlier in the chapter. Also, for each of the treatments, treatment outcome effects with conduct disorder youths have been demonstrated in randomized controlled clinical trials and replicated in multiple studies. This represents an important advance for the treatment of conduct disorder, and indeed, for child and adolescent psychotherapy more generally. Other studies might be cited for the treatment of conduct disorder because of their individual contributions and promise, even though they do not meet the criteria noted here. One illustration conveys that the richness of the outcome literature extends beyond those treatments that were reviewed.

Feldman, Caplinger, and Wodarski (1983) conducted a large-scale program that was integrated with the activities of community center that youths attended outside of school. The study included approximately 700 youths (ages 8 to 17) who were referred for antisocial behavior (referred youths) or who normally attended the regular activities programs and had not been identified as showing problem behavior (nonreferred youths). The study evaluated the effects of three types of treatment, two levels of therapist experience, and three different ways to compose the groups. The three treatments were traditional group social work (i.e., focus on group processes, social organization, and norms within the group), behavior modification (i.e., use of reinforcement contingencies, focus on prosocial behavior), and minimal treatment (i.e., no explicit application of a structured treatment plan, spontaneous interactions of group members). Activity groups within the center were formed and assigned to one of these three interventions. The groups were led by trainers, some of whom were experienced (graduate students of social work with previous experience) and others who were inexperienced (undergraduate students). Finally, the groups were composed in one of three ways: All members were youths referred for antisocial behavior; all members were nonreferred ("normal") youths; and members were a mixture of referred and nonreferred youths. The intervention was conducted over a period of a year in which the youths attended sessions and engaged in a broad range of activities (e.g., sports, arts and crafts, fund-raising, discussions). The specific treatments were superimposed on the usual activity structure of the community facility. Treatment sessions ranged from 8 to 29 sessions ($M = 22.2$ sessions) each lasting about 2 to 3 hours.

The results indicated that treatment, trainer experience, and group composition exerted impact on antisocial behavior. Youths showed greater reductions in antisocial behavior with experienced rather than inexperienced leaders. Referred (antisocial) youths in mixed groups (which included nonreferred children) showed greater improvements than similar youths in groups comprising only conduct disorder youths. Treatments also differed with behavior modification, showing greater reductions in antisocial behavior than traditional group treatment. Traditional treatment led to some decrements in behavior relative to the minimal contact group. However, treatment differences were not great in relation to outcome. Overall, the youths in the program, especially in the highly favorable intervention condition (i.e., with an experienced leader, receiving behavior modification, and in a mixed group of referred and nonreferred peers) benefited. One-year follow-up data were obtained for a only small sample of youths (less than 15%) so it was not possible to determine whether treatment effects were maintained or how the vast majority of the youths fared.

Perhaps the most critical finding is that the type of peers included in group therapies affected outcome. Conduct disorder youths in groups with other conduct disorder youths did not get better; those placed in groups with nonantisocial youths (without clinical problems) did improve. Interpretation of this is based on the likelihood that peer bonding to others can improve one's behavior if those peers engage in more normative behavior and that bonding to a deviant group can sustain deviant behavior. This is noteworthy because much of current treatments for conduct disorder youths in such settings as hospitals, schools, correctional facilities, and outpatient services is conducted in group therapy format. In such a format, several conduct problem youths come together to talk about or work on their problems, or go on outings for fresh experiences. The findings of Feldman (1992) suggest that placing several conduct disorder youths together is likely to impede therapeutic change. The importance of peers in treatment outcome in this study was suggested by the finding that within different groups, the single best predictor of change is prior behavior change of peers in the group. Overall, the project shows that interventions can be delivered on a relatively large scale and can provide benefits for referred (and nonreferred) youths in community settings.

General Comments

The techniques discussed earlier do not exhaust the available options. A multiplicity of techniques such as individual and group psychotherapy, pharmacotherapy, behavior therapy, residential treatment, and others have been applied. Presently, little evidence is available to suggest that these techniques effectively alter conduct disorder in children and adolescents. Although the data are sparse for the treatments for conduct disorder, it would be a mistake to characterize the status of all treatments in the same way.

There are a few generalities that a review of the outcome research supports for particular types of treatment. For example, *individual and group therapies* have not been well tested. *Family therapies,* excluding the version highlighted earlier, have rarely been tested in controlled outcome studies in which the identified patient is an antisocial child. In contrast, *behavior therapies* have a rather extensive literature showing that various techniques (e.g., reinforcement programs, social skills training) can alter aggressive and other antisocial behaviors. Yet the focus has tended to be on isolated behaviors rather than a constellation of symptoms. Also, durable changes among clinical samples have been rarely shown.

Pharmacotherapy represents a line of work of some interest. For one reason, stimulant medication (e.g., methylphenidate), frequently used with children diagnosed with Attention-Deficit/Hyperactivity Disorder, has some impact on aggressive and other antisocial behaviors (Hinshaw, 1991; Hinshaw, Heller, & McHale, 1992). This is interesting in part because such children often have a comorbid diagnosis of Conduct Disorder. Still no strong evidence exists that stimulant medication can alter the constellation of symptoms (e.g., fighting, stealing) associated with conduct disorder. A recent review of various medications for aggression in children and adolescents has raised possible leads, but controlled studies on the treatment of aggressive behavior specifically or on conduct disorder in general remain to be conducted (Stewart, Myers, Burket, & Lyles, 1990). Even so, at this point all leads deserve attention precisely because few treatment answers are available.

There is a genre of interventions that are worth mentioning but are even less well evaluated than many of the psychotherapies and pharmacotherapies. Occasionally, interventions are advocated and implemented such as sending conduct disorder youths to a camp in the country where they learn how to "rough it," or to take care of horses, or to experience military (e.g., basic training) regimens. The conceptual bases of such treatments, research identifying processes involved in the onset of conduct disorders and related criteria, noted earlier in the chapter are rarely even approximated with this genre of interventions. Typically such programs are not empirically evaluated. On the one hand, developing treatments that emerge outside of the mainstream of mental health is to be encouraged precisely because traditional treatments have not resolved in the problem. On the other hand, this genre of intervention tends to avoid evaluation. Evaluation is key because well-intentioned and costly interventions can have little or no effect on the youths they treat (Weisz et al., 1990). Furthermore, as will be discussed later (in Chapter 6), some interventions may actually increase antisocial behaviors (e.g., see Lundman, 1984).

SALIENT ISSUES IN TREATMENT RESEARCH

Fundamental issues are important to note in developing effective treatments for conduct disorder youths. The issues relate to the type of treatments one develops, their foci, and how to evaluate their impact. A few of these issues will be considered.

Magnitude of Therapeutic Change

Promising treatments noted previously have achieved change, but is the change enough to have impact on the lives of the treated youths and thus to make a difference in everyday life? The notion of *clinical significance* refers to the practical value or importance of the effect of an intervention, that is, whether it makes any "real" difference to the clients or to others and can be measured in many ways (see Kazdin, 1992a). One way to evaluate clinical significance is to consider the extent to which treated youths function in comparison to normative levels. Normative levels here refers to the levels of peers of the same age and sex who are functioning adequately or well in everyday life. For example, we would want treated individuals to return to school and not to get into fights or arguments, not to be placed on detention or suspended, and to be at levels in these behaviors similar to their peers functioning well in everyday life. On the positive side, we would want treated youths also to be at normative levels in their prosocial functioning, as reflected by engaging in social activities with others. Research has shown that treatments can return individuals to normative levels but that this is not necessarily true for most of the youths who are treated, even with some of the more promising treatments (e.g., Kazdin, 1993; Patterson et al., 1993).

Even seemingly marked changes may still not be sufficient in treatment. For example, in one case familiar to me, treatment reduced the number of times a 12-year-old boy sexually assaulted girls within the hospital. (The boy was under full-time supervision, but was able to escape for brief periods.) Treatment seemed to reduce these assaults from about 30 to 2 times per month. Yet his most recent episode was the fondling and attempted rape of a female patient in a closet. Assuming that treatment was responsible for the reduction in assaults, and that the assessments were reliable, we would nonetheless want greater change than this for treatment to be considered effective.

In a less dramatic case, treatment eliminated the extent to which a 10-year-old boy hit school personnel. He still was extremely verbally aggressive and this led to its own consequences (e.g., he was suspended for angrily calling the school principal a "big fat pig"). The issue here is about the goals of treatment. What can be achieved with current treatments and what are the appropriate goals? One might argue for more modest goals. For example, presumably some youths, if left untreated, would become worse. For these individuals, an important treatment effect would be preventing them from becoming worse.

In general, the magnitude of change is very important in evaluating treatment. We not only want to achieve change, we are also interested in achieving gains that make a difference in the lives of the individuals who are treated, for those with whom they are in contact, and for society at large. Because most studies of treatment have not examined whether youths have changed in ways that place them within the normative range of functioning, it is difficult to address the question.

Maintenance of Change

Much more information is needed about the long-term effects of treatment. Most studies do not report follow-up data on how well they are doing long after treatment. Among the studies that do include follow-up, assessment typically takes place 5 to 6 months after treatment ends (Kazdin, Bass, Ayers, & Rodgers, 1990). Follow-up assessment is critically important because changes immediately after treatment may not be maintained. Also, when two (or more) treatments are compared, the treatment that is more (or most) effective immediately after treatment is not always the one that proves to be the most effective treatment in the long run (Kazdin, 1988). Consequently, the conclusions about treatment may be very different depending on the timing of outcome assessment. Apart from conclusions about treatment, follow-up may provide important information that permits differentiation among youths. Over time, youths who maintain the benefits of treatment may differ in important ways from those who do not. Understanding who responds and who responds more or less well to a particular treatment can be very helpful in understanding, treating, and preventing conduct disorder.

The study of long-term effects of treatment is difficult. Families of conduct disorder youths have high rates of dropping out during treatment and during the follow-up assessment period after completion of treatment. As the sample size decreases over time, conclusions about the impact of treatment become increasingly difficult to draw. Nevertheless, evaluation of the long-term effects of treatment remains a high priority for research.

Other Issues

There remain several other issues. The criteria used to evaluate treatment is one that raises many questions. The usual focus on child symptoms is obviously important. However, most studies fail to assess or treat other domains such as prosocial behavior and academic functioning, which relate to concurrent and long-term adjustment (Kazdin et al., 1990). It is important to include in treatment evaluation a broader range of child functioning than merely symptoms.

Beyond child functioning, parent and family functioning may also be relevant. Parents and family members of conduct disorder youths often experience dysfunction (e.g., psychiatric impairment, marital conflict). Parent and family functioning and the quality of life for family members are relevant outcomes; these may be affected by treatment and are appropriate goals for treatment. Moreover, it may be necessary to focus on parent and family functioning to enhance treatment directed to the child.

In general, there are many outcomes that are of interest in evaluating treatment. From existing research we already know that the conclusions reached about a given treatment can vary depending on the outcome criterion. Within a given study, one set of measures (e.g., child functioning) may show no differences between two treatments, but another measure (e.g., family functioning) may show that one treatment is clearly better than the other (e.g., Kazdin et al., 1992; Szapocznik et al., 1989). Thus, in examining different outcomes of interest, we must be prepared for different conclusions that these outcomes may yield about treatment.

SUMMARY AND CONCLUSIONS

Many different types of treatment have been applied to conduct disorder youths. Unfortunately, little outcome evidence exists for most of the techniques. Four treatments with the most promising evidence to date have been highlighted: problem-solving skills training, parent management training, functional family therapy, and multisystemic therapy. *Cognitive problem-solving skills training* focuses on cognitive processes that underlie social behavior. *Parent management training* is directed at altering parent-child interactions in the home, particularly those interactions related to child-rearing practices and coercive interchanges. *Functional family therapy* uses principles of systems theory and behavior modification as the basis for altering interactions, communication, and problem solving among family members. *Multisystemic therapy* focuses on individual, family, and extrafamilial systems and their interrelations to develop prosocial behavior. Multiple techniques may be used to address domains contributing to antisocial behavior. Evidence relating to these interventions was reviewed; each intervention has multiple controlled studies in its behalf and some of the techniques (e.g., PMT) have been extraordinarily well evaluated.

Significant issues remain to be addressed to accelerate advances in the area of treatment. The magnitude of change and durability of treatment effects raise multiple issues about how to evaluate treatment and the conclusions reached about any particular intervention. As good as much of the evidence is, we cannot say that one intervention can ameliorate conduct disorder and overcome the poor long-term prognosis. On the other hand, much can be said. Much of what is practiced in clinical settings is based on general relationship counseling, psychodynamically oriented treatment, family therapy, and group therapy (with antisocial youths as members). These and other procedures have not been evaluated carefully in controlled trials and might be used less frequently than other techniques with established evidence.

The breadth of dysfunctions of conduct disorder youth and their families makes the task of developing effective treatments demanding. The conceptual connections between current treatment practices and the clinical dysfunctions they can be reasonably expected to alter need to be made explicit. The fact that only a few promising treatments have been identified is not cause for despair. An alternative or rather complementary approach to have impact on the problem is to intervene early, before the full disorder or constellation of symptoms has crystallized. The next chapter focuses on prevention and the efforts to intervene early. In addition, the final chapter suggests that the optimal way to intervene (treatment or prevention) with conduct disorder youths might differ from the current ways of delivering care.

NOTE

1. The number of treatment techniques available for conduct disorder is vast. The present section highlights promising approaches. Where available, literature reviews of major treatments for conduct disorder as well as for the individual treatments highlighted in this discussion are cited for the reader interested in further information.

5

PREVENTION

Prevention programs are designed to avert a problem so that it does not occur. Averting the conduct disorder problem is very attractive because it affects so many individuals, it is difficult to treat, it involves multiple problems (i.e., of the child, parents, and family), and it has exorbitant costs to society. As in the case of treatment, many different types of interventions have been implemented to prevent conduct disorder (McCord & Tremblay, 1992; U.S. Congress, 1991). Selected programs have indicated significant long-term gains, but there are complexities and nuances of prevention that make that task not as simple as one might hope. In this chapter, several types of prevention programs are illustrated to convey what has been accomplished to date.

OVERVIEW AND RATIONALE

Underlying Rationale

The limitations of treatment serve as one broad impetus for developing prevention. Treatments for conduct disorder (and for other child and adolescent mental health problems), in the form of psychotherapy, psychiatric hospitalization, and detention, are inefficient and expensive. Indeed, for many conduct disorder youths, multiple interventions are likely to be used (treatment, special education, incarceration) over the course of their lives. Also, because many treatments (e.g., psychotherapy) are provided individually, they can reach only a small portion of those in need. In fact, in the United States, approximately two thirds of children and adolescents in need of treatment do not receive services (U.S. Congress, 1991). Part of this is due to the failure to seek or use available services and due to the lack of insurance to cover services. If all youths in need actually sought treatment, the number of available mental health service providers would be grossly inadequate.

The task of treatment is very difficult. By the time mental or physical health problems (e.g., drug abuse, conduct disorder) are severe enough to warrant treatment, they may be difficult to treat (Weissberg, Caplan, & Harwood, 1991). Such problems may have already impaired the individual's functioning, making the intervention task more difficult. For these reasons, a treatment focus raises obstacles that might be overcome with effective preventive interventions.

The underpinnings of prevention extend beyond concerns about the costs and limits of treatment. The model of treatment is to focus on "problems." Prevention focuses more on building social competence and resilience as a way to promote adaptive functioning. The distinction is sometimes conveyed by noting that treatment tends to focus on "mental illness," whereas prevention focuses on "mental health." The former is oriented toward reducing or eliminating dysfunction; the latter toward developing adaptive, positive prosocial functioning. The distinction is useful as a point of departure, but too simplistic due to the interrelation of mental health and illness, the simplicity of the terms health and illness, and the broad effects that treatment and prevention programs sometimes have. Nevertheless, the point is critical because many prevention programs are designed to develop social competences that will help prevent or reduce the effects of many problems rather than the surgical focus on just averting conduct disorder or another problem. Prevention provides special opportunities not readily available with treatment. These include the possibility of reaching a large number of youths, of intervening early to reduce the number of new cases (incidence) of conduct disorder, and of promoting adaptive functioning to help avert multiple problems.

Scope of Prevention Programs

The scope of interventions designed to improve mental health and to prevent dysfunction of children and adolescents is vast in light of the many distinguishing characteristics of the programs and their objectives (Rickel & Allen, 1987; U.S. Congress, 1991). First, different goals of preventive efforts can be distinguished. *Primary prevention* consists of those interventions designed to prevent the development of psychological disorder and to promote the well-being of persons who are as yet unaffected by the dysfunction. Typically, interventions are provided to groups of persons who do not experience adjustment problems. *Secondary prevention* focuses on those persons who already show some early, mild, or moderate signs of dysfunction or are at risk for the clinical problem. Interventions are designed to stop the dysfunction from becoming worse. The distinction is often blurred because, in a given program, both adequately functioning and high-risk children may be included. For the adjusted children, the intervention is clearly directed toward primary prevention; for the high-risk children, the intervention is usually directed toward secondary prevention.[1]

Second, programs differ in their central focus. Some programs are aimed at developing prosocial competence or adaptive functioning; others focus on reducing onset of dysfunction or preventing a specific problem (e.g., substance abuse, suicide). Generally, programs tend to focus on reducing risk factors (e.g., low child IQ, harsh discipline practices) and on building protective and adaptive factors (e.g., stronger mother-child attachment, child bonding to family and school). These are not random foci, but are based on views about the processes that are considered to mediate (or lead to) dysfunction.

Third, programs vary in how and to whom they are applied. So-called *universal programs* are applied to total populations or to unselected samples of youths rather than only to those considered at risk. Thus all students in a school, district, or city might receive a universal intervention and later be evaluated to determine the impact. *Selected interventions* are those that are directed to individuals identified as high risk. Universal and selected interventions vary in their advantages (e.g., cost, risk of labeling individuals), but both are viewed as important.

Fourth, programs rely on different settings and hence on the resources and interventions deployed to achieve their goals. For example, programs in the schools, at home, and at special day care or activity centers (alone and in various combinations) have all served as the basis for prevention. Other programs are not conducted in settings in the usual way but rather rely on mass media campaigns (e.g., antismoking, antidrug use, protection against sexually transmitted diseases). These characteristics lead to a broad range of interventions and provide multiple options to improve adjustment and to prevent maladjustment.

The effectiveness of prevention programs has been evident in many areas of child and adolescent functioning (see Goldston, Yager, Heinicke, & Pynoos, 1990; Price, Cowen, Lorion, & Ramos-McKay, 1988; Rickel & Allen, 1987), including conduct disorder and delinquency (see McCord

& Tremblay, 1992; Zigler, Taussig, & Black, 1992). Prevention programs directed early in life (e.g., pre- and postnatal counseling, continued contact with family and child in first few years of life), as well as throughout childhood and adolescence, have been shown to reduce risk for maladaptive behaviors (e.g., school dropout, antisocial behavior) and clinical dysfunction. However, the conclusions about prevention programs require more focused scrutiny to convey nuances, challenges, and current limitations. Different types of programs are used to illustrate the focus of prevention. As in the treatment chapter, this chapter will selectively review promising programs.

PROMISING PREVENTION PROGRAMS

Early Parent/Family Intervention

Perhaps the most obvious question for prevention is when to intervene. In the case of conduct disorder, perhaps the answer is also obvious —before the child is born. The reason is that risk factors for conduct disorder, such as characteristics of parents and family (e.g., history of conduct disorder, currently large family size, socioeconomic disadvantage, high stress) can be identified before birth of the child. Also, other risk factors (e.g., teenage pregnancy of the mother, prenatal and perinatal complications) cannot await intervention until the child is born. Consequently, many prevention programs begin before the child is born and continue throughout the first few years of the child's life (e.g., Meisels & Shonkoff, 1990). Several studies have focused on the reduction of risk factors that portend child and family dysfunction, including child conduct disorder. In many of these studies, the purpose was not to prevent conduct disorder of the children; nor were measures of conduct disorder included to evaluate program outcome. Nevertheless, the connection between risk reduction and conduct disorder is evident in a few studies; these convey the relevance of this focus.

A noteworthy primary prevention program was designed to improve women's prenatal health habits, infant caregiving, social support, use of community services, and educational and career work so they could decrease reliance on welfare (Olds, 1988). The focus on maternal health and reduction of childhood disorders (e.g., prematurity and low birth weight) was predicted to have broader effects, as reflected in behavioral problems of the children and parental child abuse. Although the specific goals did not include the prevention of child conduct disorder, the focus on child birth weight, maternal care, and child-rearing practices are quite squarely within the domain of risk factors for conduct disorder.

The focus was on mothers who were at risk, as defined by being relatively young (i.e., less than 19 years old), single, or low socioeconomic status. Women with at least one of these characteristics from a semirural community were selected and assigned to an intervention group or to a minimal intervention group. The intervention group received home visits by nurses beginning when the women were pregnant and continuing over a period of 2 years. The intervention and its goals varied at different points in time. As an illustration, during pregnancy, mothers were instructed to help improve their diets, to reduce the use of alcohol, drugs, and cigarettes, to maintain personal hygiene and to exercise. After the child's birth, home visits focused on parental understanding of child temperament, child cognitive development, and diverse facets of functioning related to the mother's and child's well-being. Mothers in the minimal intervention group received a few services (e.g., transportation, well child care services) but not the extensive home visit program. At the child's second birthday, the intervention ended. Children were followed 2 years later.

In comparison to those who had received minimal services, mothers who had received the intervention reduced their cigarette smoking, had babies with higher birth weights, showed fewer cases of child abuse and neglect, and had fewer emergency room visits with their children. In terms of the mothers' own lives, the women who received the intervention had higher levels of employment and fewer pregnancies than the minimal intervention group. These results convey that a "family" of risk factors related to conduct disorder (i.e., child birth complications, child abuse, welfare status, large family size) can be altered by an intensive intervention aimed at young mothers.

In another project, young economically disadvantaged parents received an intervention designed to support the development of their children and to improve family life (Provence & Naylor, 1983). The rationale was that impairment and stress of the parents impedes family functioning and increases risk of dysfunction for the child. Mothers at the poverty level were recruited for the project. After the project was completed, a sample matched on several variables (e.g., income level, parents in the home, ethnicity) were recruited and served as a nonintervention control group. The intervention consisted of services to the mothers for a period of 2½ years after delivery. These included home visits by a social worker to address various needs (e.g., safety, obtaining adequate financial and housing aid), child visits for day care at the program center, and developmental and pediatric exams of the child. Within the structure of the program and contacts with program staff, services were tailored to the needs of individual families.

For present purposes, the 10-year follow-up data are particularly interesting (Seitz, Rosenbaum, & Apfel, 1985). In comparison to control mothers, mothers who had received the intervention were more likely to be self-employed, to have had fewer children, and to have spaced the births of their children more widely. Birth rate and spacing of children (i.e., density of the family or family size) address the risk factors that were noted earlier for conduct disorder. Children of parents in the intervention group showed higher rates of school attendance, required fewer special services, and were rated more positively by their teachers. Ratings by teachers reflected less aggression, fewer acting out behaviors (a condition of special classroom placement), and fewer school suspensions. Mothers in the control reported more antisocial behaviors in their children (such as staying out all night without maternal knowledge, cruelty to animals, and aggressive behavior toward parents and siblings). This study is significant in demonstrating direct changes in risk factors for conduct disorder, reductions in antisocial behavior, and long-term consequences of early intervention.

An early intervention program was evaluated for economically disadvantaged mothers who were recruited in the last trimester of pregnancy (Lally, Mangione, & Honig, 1988). The intervention consisted of contact with paraprofessionals who provided diverse services related to mother and child care (e.g., nutrition, child development, improvements in parent-child interactions, assistance with community services, and other features). Home visits were provided weekly to assist families with such issues as child rearing, family relations, employment, and community functioning. Although parent contact was viewed as the primary intervention, a central part of the program was day care; this was provided to the children for approximately 5 years. Intervention families were compared to a nonrandomly composed control group selected in the same way as the intervention group and matched on several subject and demographic variables.

Follow-up evaluation was completed 10 years after the program had ended when the children were between 13 and 16 years of age. Among the changes, those related to conduct disorder are particularly noteworthy. Youths in the intervention group showed fewer instances of probation, less severity of recorded offenses, lower degree of chronicity, and lower costs (e.g., court costs, probation, placement, detention, and related costs) than youths in the control group. Thus the early intervention had a direct impact on conduct disorder.

As a final illustration, an early intervention program was designed to reduce academic disadvantage and prevent behavioral problems among young Mexican American children (Johnson, 1988). The subjects were 1-year-old children who had not yet evinced behavioral problems. Poverty and minority status of the families served as risk and inclusion factors. Families were recruited annually over a period of 8 years and assigned randomly to intervention or nonintervention control conditions.

The intervention began when the children were age 1 and ended when they were age 3. Central features of the intervention included home visits with mothers to increase understanding of child care and development; personal counseling; family weekly activities (e.g., workshops, social events); activities at the program center where children attended nursery school; and sessions for mothers dealing with child academic tasks, child problem behavior, and home management issues (e.g., budgeting). Extensive efforts were made to involve the entire family, to address a broad range of issues related to child rearing and child development, and to respond to the diverse interests of the parents (e.g., driver education, sex education, family planning).

Follow-up assessment was conducted 5 to 8 years after the program had been completed; at that time, the children were in the second and third grades. Results indicated that acting out behavior in the classroom was significantly more common for control children than for intervention children. Four times as many children in the control group were referred for special services. Children in the intervention group also performed better than controls on several measures of cognitive and intellectual skills.

School-Based Interventions

The early parent/family-based interventions emphasized maternal care and early child development. These programs also included day care and early school-related experiences for children. Several interventions relevant to conduct disorder have focused primarily on school-based interventions; often these were supplemented by additional contacts with the parents.

A program that has received considerable attention was designed to help children at risk for school failure (Schweinhart & Weikart, 1988; Weikart & Schweinhart, 1987, 1992). Risk of school failure was based on parental lack of education, low family income, and a stressful environment. The study began with 3- to 4-year-old children who were randomly assigned to intervention or nonintervention groups. The intervention included a classroom program for a period of 2 years. The program for the children occurred 5 mornings per week for 7 months each year. Weekly teacher visits to the children's homes were also included during this period. Curricula and teacher-child activities were designed to address diverse needs (e.g., intellectual, social, physical) guided by Piagetian views of development of decision making and other cognitive processes.

The program ended when the children were between 5 and 6 years of age. Follow-up assessments continued over several years. The follow-up at age 19 years conveyed several noteworthy findings: Youths who had participated in the preschool program had lower levels of mental retardation, of dropping out of school, and of reliance on welfare than the youths in the nonintervention group. They also showed greater literacy, higher levels of employment, and greater attendance at college or vocational school. At age 19, women who as youths received the preschool program reported fewer pregnancies and births than women who had not received the program. Thus the program altered a variety of risk factors in the index youths for their own offspring (e.g., family size, education, and, presumably, social class as a result of employment status). Of special significance for present purposes are the data on conduct disorder. On self-report measures and arrest records, youths who participated in the program showed lower rates of antisocial behavior. More specifically, fewer youths who received the intervention had come to the attention of juvenile authorities or had ever been arrested.

In another school-based program, Hawkins and his colleagues (Hawkins et al., 1992; Hawkins, Doueck, & Lishner, 1988) focused specifically on curbing conduct disorder. The program focused on increasing opportunities, skills, and rewards of the children in an effort to develop prosocial bonding to conventional social institutions (e.g., family, school, peer relations) and values. The intervention included multiple components. The classroom and school components focused on classroom management to address deportment, interactive teaching, and cooperative learning techniques (involving peers). Each of these was directed toward increasing the children's involvement in the class and their attachment to teachers and nondeviant peers. The classroom programs altered the environment to support appropriate behavior, academic skills, and interpersonal attachments to others. A family-based component (e.g., parent management training) was designed to improve family management skills and to assist in conflict resolution in relation to misconduct at home and at school. Other components included peer-focused social skills training and community-focused interventions in which career education and counseling were introduced.

The program has been ongoing with cohorts enrolled at different points in time and assigned randomly to intervention or nonintervention conditions. Data available at the end of the first year of the program indicated that youths receiving intervention showed fewer suspensions and expulsions from school than nonintervention youths. Subsequent evaluations have shown reduced rates of self-reported delinquency (e.g., truancy, theft) and alcohol use among fifth-grade youths exposed to a comprehensive program during Grades 1 to 4. Moreover, analyses have shown that processes considered to mediate intervention effects (e.g., bonding to family and school) change over the course of the intervention (Hawkins et al., 1992).

An interesting focus has emphasized the adaptation of students as they move from one school to another (Felner & Adan, 1988). The program is based on findings that transitions from one school to the next are associated with decreases in academic performance and with increases in deportment and psychological symptoms, including conduct disorder. Transitions may increase vulnerability to dysfunction because of the stress they induce and because of varying skills of individuals to cope with the stress.

Felner and Adan (1988) devised the School Transitional Environmental Program (STEP) to facilitate the adaptation of students during the process of school transitions. Transitions refer to the normal process of entering a new school (e.g., from middle to high school). The STEP program sought to reduce difficult transitions and to increase coping responses. Two major components defined the program. First, an effort was made to reorganize the new school social system so that students were involved in a stable peer group. Other features were structured to create a more consistent environment than would ordinarily would be the case (e.g., classes with a common group, classes in close proximity to each other). Second, the program redefined the role of the homeroom teacher as a primary administrator and a counselor for students. This person worked with individual children, served as a resource for school and family issues, and provided special counseling sessions, as needed, during homeroom periods.

In one of a number evaluations of the program, the focus was on a large urban high school with students entering the ninth grade from low socioeconomic and minority families (Felner & Adan, 1988). The program was invoked for the first (transitional) year of school; when this year was completed, students entered the general student population. At the end of the first year, control students matched to the STEP students but not receiving intervention showed decreases in academic performance and increases in absenteeism; STEP students did not. Follow-up data indicated that the STEP students had lower rates of dropping out and of placements in alternative programs for failing students. STEP students also showed higher grades and fewer absences than the control students during the first and second year of high school. By the third and fourth year of high school, the differences between control and STEP youths were less evident, possibly due in part to the higher dropout rates of the control youths by this time.

The STEP program has been replicated and extended to a broad range of outcome measures (see Felner & Adan, 1988). The replications have been conducted in high schools and junior high schools and in rural and suburban communities. One- or 2-year follow-up data, depending upon different cohorts, demonstrated the program's impact on academic performance and on emotional and behavioral dysfunction. Substance abuse and delinquent activity were favorably affected by the STEP youths in comparisons with control youths. The ongoing evaluation of this program precludes definitive and long-term conclusions of greater specificity at this time. However, the currently available results convey impact directly relevant to conduct disorder.

A novel school-based program was conducted in Norway as part of a nationwide intervention aimed at decreasing aggressive behavior (or "bullying") in the schools (Olweus, 1991). Bullying referred to repeated victimization (e.g., verbal or physical aggression) by one's peers who had a power differential of some type (e.g., a difference in strength, age, or status). The program was applied to youths in the Grades 1 through 9. The intervention encompassed teachers, parents, and students. Written materials and other sources of information (e.g., a videocassette) were provided to teachers and parents, and other efforts were made to increase knowledge about the problem of bullying. Within the school, rules were provided and enforced regarding bullying, and efforts were made to support and protect victims. The large-scale effort and the mobilization of multiple influences across settings at micro and macro levels are unique strengths of this program.

The program's impact was evaluated in a quasi-experimental design involving separate cohorts of students (see Olweus, 1991). After 2 years of the program, bullying was reduced by 50% or more across all grades. Effects were evident for both boys and girls. In addition, several antisocial behaviors such as theft, vandalism, and truancy, which were not focused on directly, decreased as well. The program is worth highlighting as an intervention because it conveys an effort to institutionalize an intervention and to deploy teachers, parents, and students in a consistent and concentrated fashion.

Community-Based Interventions

Community-based interventions use existing facilities in the community (e.g., recreational centers, parks) or bring intervention to youths in the contexts of their everyday lives. These interventions take advantage of the resources in the everyday environment that can support prosocial behavior. Thus community-based programs are often conducted in local recreational or youth centers in which activity programs are already underway. Integration of programs in the community also helps to promote the carryover of prosocial behavior to everyday situations because the intervention is conducted in these situations rather than in special and more restricted settings (e.g., psychiatric hospitals, juvenile correctional facilities).

For example, Fo and O'Donnell (1975; O'Donnell, 1992; O'Donnell, Lygate, & Fo, 1979) conducted programs for youths (ages 11 to 17) referred from a number of agencies (public schools, courts, social welfare agencies) for their behavioral and academic problems. Some of the youths who participated had prior arrest records; others did not. Hence the project at once addressed treatment (remediation of adjudicated youths) and prevention (for those at risk for delinquency). Adults were recruited from the community to work as therapists and to conduct behavior modification programs individually with the youths. They met with the youths, engaged in a variety of activities (e.g., arts and crafts, fishing, camping), and implemented and evaluated a behavior modification program. Individualized reward programs focused on such behaviors as truancy, fighting, completing chores at home, and doing homework.

The study found different rates of truancy, fighting, staying out late, and other problem behaviors in relation to control youths who did not receive treatment. Also, over a 2-year follow-up period, arrest records reflected gains in treated youths relative to nontreatment controls. However, the effects of the program varied as a function of whether the children had a prior record of offenses. Youths who completed the program and who had no prior arrest records became worse with the intervention, as reflected by an increase in rates of major offenses. This finding might be due to the increased friendships and relationships of less deviant youths with more deviant peers that occurred during the project period as a result of the multiple opportunities for contacts and socialization (O'Donnell, 1992). The program was effective, however, in decreasing antisocial behavior among those youths who initially had more severe arrest records.

Among community-based interventions, those devoted to curbing recidivism with individuals early in their career are particularly noteworthy. Davidson and his colleagues (Davidson & Redner, 1988; Davidson, Redner, Blakely, Mitchell, & Emshoff, 1987) have developed such a program for youths (12 to 16 years old) who have been identified as delinquent. The program was designed for youths who had been apprehended and referred to juvenile courts but who had not been formally adjudicated. Most youths in recent demonstrations were referred for property related offenses (e.g., breaking and entering, larceny, auto theft).

The intervention consisted of close contact of the individual youth with a college student volunteer. The volunteer was trained and supervised by graduate students who were in turn supervised by university faculty. The student and youth were in close contact (6 to 8 hours per week) for 18 weeks. The intervention included behavioral contracting, child advocacy, help for the youth to obtain access to community resources, and involvement in the community. The contacts between the student volunteer and the youth took place in the youth's home, in recreational settings, or in other convenient locales as needed. Carefully controlled and large-scale evaluations of the diversion program showed that the intervention reduced recidivism among those who participated. Recidivism rates reflected police contacts up to 2 years after the point of intake (Davidson et al., 1987).

There are several notable features of this program, including the replication of intervention effects in several studies and the comparison of the intervention to diverse controls (e.g., attention-placebo) and to alternative intervention conditions (e.g., traditional court processing). Also, the program has evaluated alternative types of settings and volunteers (e.g., college students, community members) and staff (e.g., paid social workers). These results suggest a viable and well-replicated intervention for reducing severity of dysfunction in youths apprehended for offenses.

Impact of Interventions: Overall Evaluation

Evidence from the studies mentioned earlier, as well as others that might be cited (e.g., McCord & Tremblay, 1992; Yoshikawa, 1994; Zigler et al., 1992) indicate that prevention programs have reduced the onset of conduct disorder. The outcomes have included reductions in aggression toward parents and siblings, truancy, cruelty, school suspensions and expulsions, substance abuse, and delinquency (as measured by self-report and arrest records). Evidence also indicates that early interventions can reduce multiple factors that place youths at risk for conduct disorder, including birth complications of mothers, birth rate (and hence family size), abusive child-rearing practices, family reliance on welfare, and poor academic performance and educational levels of children and their mothers. As noted previously, in many of the studies, the purpose was not to demonstrate that changes in these factors reduced conduct disorder. Yet the evidence that these factors increase risk for conduct disorder and that reduction of such factors in a few studies in fact decreased antisocial behavior establishes the significance of risk reduction as a means of preventing conduct disorder.

Within the studies cited, several qualifiers limit the strength of the conclusions. First, the long-term impact of prevention interventions is not well studied. Many of the studies focus on changes while the program is in effect, or 1 or 2 years later. Thus firm conclusions about the impact of interventions up to, say, 10 years later, cannot generally be made with confidence. Second and related, few studies directly focus on conduct disorder as an outcome. The absence of a direct focus in many studies means that few measures related specifically to conduct disorder are included. Reductions in classroom misbehavior or self-reported delinquent acts are important. However, evaluation of program efficacy requires assessment of multiple measures of conduct disorder to encompass performance in different settings (e.g., home, school, community), to encompass different sources of information (e.g., self, parent, teachers), and to encompass different methods of assessment (e.g., self-report measures, institutional records). Absent more comprehensive assessment, our knowledge of the impact of preventive programs on conduct disorder is limited to a small number of programs.

Third, little is known about the critical components that produce change. The bulk of research has compared intervention versus nonintervention conditions. This comparison is quite understandable given the priority of demonstrating the effects of an intervention package. At the same time, comparisons are required to further analyze components and parameters of treatment and their impact. The heavy reliance on intervention versus nonintervention comparisons raises other issues. Participation in a "special prevention" program, apart from the content of the intervention has potential impact yet to be well documented. Very special arrangements and delineation of a project in the schools or home mean that the intervention group has special demands that could contribute to outcome. Small-scale evaluations of these influences as part of prevention trials would require inclusion of attention-placebo control conditions or variations of active interventions (e.g., Bien & Bry, 1980; Davidson et al., 1987; Pierson, 1988). Efforts to evaluate the special status of intervention groups and whether this contributes to change would enhance our understanding of the basis for change.

Fourth, little is known about the optimal time to intervene. Of the programs reviewed, those related to early intervention with parents and families and selected school-based programs have provided positive evidence regarding the reduction of conduct disorder. It would be tempting to make sweeping claims about the focus of those interventions and to draw implications about the need to intervene in one way (e.g., early in life in the home) rather than another (e.g., community-wide interventions). The literature does not permit one to draw statements about the best place to intervene or the relative merit of alternative foci or interventions. It may be more useful to view interventions in a developmental context insofar as risk factors for conduct disorder and points of intervention can be identified at different ages (e.g., infancy, adolescence). Opportunities for intervention are not necessarily lost even if intervention is not conducted at an earlier age.

Notwithstanding these qualifiers, current evidence has shown reliable effects in reduction of risk factors for conduct disorder and for constituent behaviors of conduct disorder. We know that early intervention with families (e.g., prenatal care, parenting instruction, and direct assistance) can have marked impact when it is continued for a few years (e.g., into the early preschool years of the child's life or longer); focused on multiple domains and risk factors (e.g., nutrition, parent-child interaction, cognitive development of the child); done in different settings (e.g., at home, day care, and school); and done among high-risk samples (e.g., socioeconomically disadvantaged). Many questions remain but the initial answer to the most basic question, "Can any intervention prevent conduct disorder?" is affirmative. The diversity of programs and the repetition of effects within individual programs provide compelling evidence that positive measures can be taken to reduce conduct disorder among families and youths at risk for dysfunction.

MAJOR ISSUES AND OBSTACLES

If we know that prevention can work, why not extend existing programs to society at large? Many impediments may come to mind, such as the cost of large-scale applications, the difficulties of infringing on individual rights depending on how programs are implemented, and the issue of individual choices in participation. Yet prior to addressing these concerns, there are fundamental issues from the evidence itself that are important to consider.

Early Identification of Youths at Risk

Obviously, a critical point of departure for preventive efforts is identifying children at risk. This task would seem to be not that difficult because the research on risk factors (highlighted earlier) revealed child, parent, family, and other (e.g., school) factors that relate to the onset of conduct disorder. Yet there are limits in using this information in identifying specific children at risk. For example, early signs of conduct disorder and unmanageability in the child is one of the predictors of later dysfunction among boys. Yet longitudinal and cross-sectional studies of development have shown that disruptive, problematic, and antisocial behaviors have relatively high prevalence rates in early childhood. These behaviors can be seen early in adjusted children whose long-term course is not likely to include conduct disorder. Among "normal" low-risk children, there is a tendency for such behaviors to decline over the course of development. Efforts to select high-risk children could inadvertently yield a large number of cases for whom such behaviors do not portend subsequent dysfunction.

Similarly, even when multiple risk factors are used in combination, they may not identify all or even most of the individuals who later show conduct disorder. Different combinations of risk factors and algorithms for their combination have been evaluated in an effort to predict who will become delinquent. For example, Farrington (1985) compared alternative methods of combining child, parent, and family variables to predict who would become delinquent. The study represented a longitudinal investigation identifying children at approximately age of 8 and following them through early adulthood. The results indicated that even with the best combination of predictors, only approximately 50% of the delinquent youths could be correctly identified. A particular problem for prevention work is the less than ideal rates for identification of *true positives* (i.e., persons who are high on the risk factors early in life and who eventually show the problem). Obviously related are the corresponding measures that reflect the problems of selection, namely, the presence of *false positives* (i.e., persons who are high on the risk factors and identified as likely to show the problem but who do not), and the presence of *false negatives* (i.e., persons who do not appear to be at risk but who eventually show the problem).

At this point, predicting who will show clinically severe antisocial behavior is quite complex, to say the least. The specific factors that serve as the best set of predictors vary as a function of the age that the child is evaluated (e.g., early or middle childhood), the criteria that are predicted (e.g., police or court contacts, conviction, self-reported delinquent acts), and the characteristics of the sample (e.g., income level of the sample determines which factors emerge as risk factors) (see Boyle & Offord, 1990; Farrington, 1985; Loeber & Dishion, 1983). Under the best circumstances, identification of high-risk children based on the many sets of variables that relate to onset of dysfunction is also likely to select significant proportions of persons who will never show the problem (i.e., false positives) and to miss others who will (i.e., false negatives).

Perhaps a significant proportion of high-risk youths will manifest disturbance in adolescence and adulthood. However, there is another proportion that will not. Moreover, many youths who are not at risk at the time a preventive effort begins and who do not receive the intervention may evince problems later (Wenar, 1984). The fact that children grow out of as well as into problems reduces the efficiency and efficacy of preventive efforts in ameliorating a particular problem.

The model of prevention often includes the application of interventions on a large scale rather than specifically with selected high-risk individuals. Thus, if conduct disorder cannot be predicted as well as one would like, perhaps it would be just as well to use the risk factors but not to be restrictive in selecting children and adolescents for intervention programs. Thus one might loosen the selection criteria with the idea of obtaining those at high risk as well as many others. Stated differently, the selection criteria can be lenient so as to minimize false negatives (youths who do not seem at risk but in fact are) at the risk of inadvertently obtaining a few more false positives (youths who are not at risk but seem to be on the selection criteria). Such a strategy might be quite defensible. However, universal and wider-scale programs can be more costly and more difficult to implement well compared with smaller scale and more focused interventions.

Effectiveness of Interventions

When we say that prevention programs have proven to be effective, what does that mean? An effective program is one demonstrating that those who received the intervention have lower rates of onset of the problem than those who did not receive that intervention. This does not necessarily mean that the problem has been completely prevented among those who received the intervention. For example, in an exemplary preschool program mentioned earlier, follow-up data were collected years later when the youths were 15 and then 19 years old (Weikart & Schweinhart, 1992). Youths in the preschool intervention group scored significantly better on several measures, including the measure "ever arrested" (31% vs. 51%); the mean number of arrests (1.3 vs. 2.3); completion of high school; and being on welfare. The intervention clearly affected the lives of many individuals. Yet the program did not eliminate arrests or being on welfare. The point of this is simple. Very effective prevention programs can still leave several individuals who have the problem (e.g., are arrested).

It is important to note that an effective prevention does not necessarily prevent the problem in everyone at risk or even necessarily among most of those who are at risk. This is not necessarily a limitation of prevention programs. The impact on a significant number of youths is important. Also, the social impact of even a mildly effective intervention can be enormous because of the scope of impact among those individuals who improved (e.g., arrest records, on welfare, high school graduation, and years of college education). These measures can continue to have lifelong consequences for the individuals themselves as well as for their offspring. The point of mentioning the fact that many or most individuals at risk may not be improved is to convey that an effective prevention program ought not to be expected to eliminate the onset of the problem.

First Do No Harm

A related issue is the potential effects of preventive efforts other than those that are intended. There has been an assumption that if preventive efforts prove ineffective, at least they will not harm. However, occasionally preventive efforts have even led to deleterious effects. Perhaps the best known example is the Cambridge-Somerville Youth Study, which was designed to prevent delinquency (Powers & Witmer, 1951). The study involved more than 500 boys, including those at risk for delinquency. The boys received either a broad-based and not very well-specified intervention (involving psychiatric and medical attention, academic assistance, repeated contact with a counselor, and community programs) or no treatment. Follow-up 30 years after treatment (McCord, 1978) revealed that those who were in the treated group had higher rates of criminal activity, alcoholism, serious disease, symptoms of stress, lower job status and satisfaction, and death at an earlier age. These adverse effects have drawn attention to the possibility that intervening may be harmful.

Other evidence has corroborated the risk of deleterious effects with preventive interventions. For example, some programs have exposed delinquent youths to adult prisoners who describe prison life, convey their own life experiences, and intimidate youths to scare them into not pursuing criminal activity. Variations of these programs (e.g., referred to as "scared straight" or "stay straight") have shown deleterious effects. Youths exposed to these programs showed increases in their subsequent rates of arrest in comparison to control youths (Buckner & Chesney-Lind, 1983; Finckenauer, 1982). Although the reason is not known, the prevailing view is that these programs bring delinquent youths into contact with each other as part of the program. These contacts lead to friendships that continue outside of the program. And, friendship with (or bonding to) deviant peers is known to be a significant deleterious influence on deviant behavior.

Preventive interventions in other areas (e.g., drug use, suicide prevention) have produced deleterious effects insofar as the group exposed to the intervention became worse (Bangert-Drowns, 1988; Shaffer et al., 1990). The occurrence of undesirable effects is infrequent and should not be used to discourage preventive efforts. The varied effects of interventions underscore the need to evaluate outcome both immediately after the intervention phase is completed and over the course of follow-up, as well as the need to understand how interventions operate (i.e., the processes through which change is produced).

Conducting Research on Prevention

There are a number of obstacles that make prevention research unusually difficult. At the outset, the initial task of any prevention research project usually is to make the case that an intervention is needed. The absence of symptoms is perceived as no problem, making the need for an intervention unpersuasive to would-be participants. Establishing the need for the intervention requires firmly convincing people of the connection between a risk factor and the ultimate problem. The case has been heavily promoted for some problems (e.g., drawing the connection to the public between hypertension—"the silent killer"—and risk of a heart attack). It may be more difficult to establish the case as readily for psychological, psychiatric, and behavioral problems.

Once the case is made convincingly that the intervention is needed, it is difficult to convey the need among participants for a nontreatment control condition. Prevention research is invariably longitudinal, so that a true test of the intervention comes from comparing the treated group with the untreated group to see in the next several years whether the conduct disorder, clinical referrals, delinquency rates, and other measures of interest decline. The nontreatment control group is usually needed to address the base rates of change over the course of development. Yet it is unclear why participants would remain in such a group if they believed that their children were truly at risk and in need of a program of some sort.

Another obstacle is the seemingly undramatic outcomes that successful prevention programs promise (Glidewell, 1983). If successful, the intervention will lead to the absence of specific problems or generally improved adjustment. One could argue that, for a particular child, the problem might not have emerged anyway. Thus the effect of the intervention is not obvious. In contrast, treatment in any given case may yield a dramatic effect, as evident in a total remission of symptoms. The "before" and "after" differences in the behavior of a successfully treated individual are highly persuasive and make the case for the potential benefits of treatment. The analogue of a successful prevention program is a "before" and "after" description in which the problem was not there to begin with and never emerged later.

There are other related issues as well. Identification of children for a prevention project can inadvertently label them as problematic or at risk. Given the prediction data, many of these children might not eventually show conduct disorder. Their early labeling as a risk introduces the potential for stigma based on reactions of teachers and peers; there is also the danger of the label becoming a self-fulfilling prophesy. In the case of a treatment study such labeling may also occur. However, in that instance, there is an identified clinical problem. Presumably, the importance of the problem to the parent usually outweighs the concern of any risks associated with labeling. The case may be different for a prevention study. Indeed, the concern for labeling and stigmatizing youths and their families has served as one of the reasons for community-wide interventions, so that no subset of youth are identified as at risk.

In brief, there are all sorts of problems related to recruitment, retention, and evaluation of participants in prevention programs. Many programs report such problems. For example, those who agree to participate in a program are often better functioning (i.e., less at risk) than those who do not agree (Levenstein, 1992); more severe cases tend to agree to participate more often in intervention conditions than in control conditions (e.g., Tremblay et al., 1992); groups at the beginning of a prevention trial are often not equivalent in severity of impairment (Hawkins, Von Cleve, & Catalano, 1991); and cases more severely at risk tend to drop out more often (Booth, Spieker, Barnard, & Morisset, 1992). These are not trivial obstacles because they have implications for the evaluation of program effectiveness and for the large-scale implementation of programs.

General Comments

In the chapter on treatment, many obstacles and difficulties were identified that have impeded high quality research. The tasks for conducting prevention research are often much more difficult. Many of the prevention studies highlighted earlier have used paraprofessionals as trainers; have conducted multifaceted programs across multiple settings (e.g., home and community) in a single investigation; and have administered assessments repeatedly over protracted periods. Obstacles associated with training therapists, maintaining integrity of treatment, and coordinating the interventions across settings are particularly acute for prevention studies. The reason is that prevention programs tend to be large scale, involving, as they do, many classrooms, schools, and cities. As the scale of the program increases, there tends to be increased difficulty in monitoring the quality of the program and its implementation among staff. In many high quality prevention programs, for example, researchers report that the program was implemented well only in some classrooms or by some of the staff (e.g., Allen, Philliber, & Hoggson, 1990; Botvin, Baker, Filazzola, & Botvin, 1990; Hawkins & Lam, 1987). Wide variations in program implementation have led to problems in evaluating the impact of the intervention (see Kazdin, 1992b). Perhaps a more critical issue is the broader concern about whether prevention programs, if implemented on a large scale, can be expected to have large-scale effects because of difficulties in maintaining the integrity of treatment. Notwithstanding these considerations, prevention programs for conduct disorder have made significant gains. Reliable reductions in a variety of antisocial behaviors among children and adolescents have been demonstrated repeatedly. The advances to date, even though qualified, have led many authors to note that we now know enough to have an impact on the problem (e.g., Olweus, 1991; Zigler et al., 1992).

SUMMARY AND CONCLUSIONS

There have been many prevention programs, particularly for children identified as at risk for later maladjustment. Several of these programs have shown positive changes in child functioning years after the intervention has been terminated. An interesting feature is that the interventions often have been implemented in the schools and communities and on a relatively large scale. Thus the technology for delivering many different interventions and for their evaluation is well established. A difficulty that pervades the literature is the somewhat generic goals of prevention programs, namely, to decrease risk for dysfunction and to improve well-being and adjustment. These goals are laudatory and significant to be sure. However, in the case of a specific interest or problem domain such as conduct disorder, conclusions are limited. As in the case of treatment, there are many promising prevention strategies. Few evaluations provide specific reference to the prevention of conduct disorder and delinquency.

Prevention of conduct disorder is a goal that continues to hold great hope. There are, however, major obstacles inherent in the enterprise that make difficult the identification and implementation of effective programs. Identification and recruitment of high-risk children or families raise special problems. These problems are not insurmountable. The scope of the effort that is needed has already been evident in selected studies in which the primary limitation has been the failure to focus on and measure antisocial behavior rather than more global measures of adjustment.

NOTE

1. *Tertiary prevention* is sometimes used to refer to interventions applied to individuals who already show the problem, although the goal might be to prevent individuals from becoming worse. The term is not used extensively in the prevention literature because this amounts to treatment or interventions for those with the problem. However, the term is useful insofar as it places prevention and treatment on a continuum of points of intervening.

6

NEW DIRECTIONS FOR RESEARCH

Considerable progress has been made in the study of conduct disorder. Improved methods of assessing child and adolescent functioning and methods of unravelling the relations among influences have contributed to the progress. Current work continuing in the usual way will no doubt lead to further progress. At the same time, additional areas of research might be pursued to expand the focus of research, to overcome limitations of current efforts to understand conduct problems, and to identify different approaches for having impact on the problem. This chapter considers lines of work designed to build on current advances.

DIAGNOSIS AND EVALUATION OF CONDUCT DISORDER

Increased Specificity in Studying Conduct Problems

Conduct Disorder, as a diagnostic category (e.g., in *DSM-IV*), refers to a rather heterogeneous class of antisocial behaviors. There is little question that a broad diagnosis can be reliably made and has use at the general level both for research (e.g., identifying risk factors) and for policy (e.g., management of youths within school settings). Yet a number of arguments might be made for greater specificity for understanding conduct disorder. First, examining global classes of heterogeneous children and adolescents may mask identification of subtypes and effective strategies for their management and treatment. For example, youths may differ widely in chronicity, age, and patterns of dysfunction. Interventions appropriate for selected subsamples may not

122

show overall effects when applied to the heterogeneous class, "conduct disorder."

Second, scrutiny of subpopulations of antisocial youths reveals major definitional problems in the identification of cases and assessment of dysfunction. For example, *truancy* or persistent absence from school is one of the symptoms of conduct disorder. Identification of truancy would seem to be straightforward because children can be selected from school records and parents can be asked about the reasons for child absenteeism. Moreover because school attendance is compulsory, detection should be facilitated. Yet the identification of truant youths is hampered by the problems in distinguishing excused from unexcused absences; in delineating unexcused absences unbeknownst to the parent from absences due to school phobia and school refusal; and in overcoming biases of clinicians in assigning the label "truant" to children because of the legal implications for the parents (e.g., fines, loss of custody) (see Galloway, 1985). The definitional issues are not academic but are at the core of understanding the clinical problem, its prevalence, characteristics, and likely points of effective intervention. The problems of defining truancy and identifying index cases derive from an intensive study of the problem rather than larger grouping of individuals in the heterogeneous class of conduct disorder.

As another example, *setting fires* is also a symptom of conduct disorder and one that also should be easy to identify because of the discrete nature of the behavior. Nonetheless, basic problems emerge at the definitional level that have critical implications for understanding the problem. What defines a firesetter? There are many alternatives, including playing with matches, lighting small fires of no consequence, and arson involving major damage or injury. The assessment of firesetting relies on reports of the child or parent. Child and parent agreement on the occurrence of firesetting is only moderate (see Kolko & Kazdin, 1992). Perhaps the limited agreement ought to be expected for fires set outside the home. In such instances, the child could be the only one in the family aware of the fire, and he may simply choose not to report it.

The ambiguities surrounding the definition and identification of symptoms that compose conduct disorder (e.g., truancy and firesetting) underscore the importance of focusing narrowly on a particular problem domain. The reason is that defining conduct disorder to include multiple problem domains (e.g., truancy, firesetting, and many other areas) merely compounds the ambiguities of who is studied, what characteristics permitted them to be included in the sample, and so on. The broad class of conduct disorder youths includes a great deal of "noise" or "error." Research has shown that even with this amount of imprecision, systematic differences can be identified—for example, when conduct disorder youths are compared to youths with other diagnoses. However, many reliable characteristics of the various subsamples of youths with conduct disorder will obscured. The factors may only be revealed when subsamples are delineated. In general, finer grained analyses of problem areas warrant greater attention. Such analyses will also capture a broader range of individuals than currently studied. For example, studying all individuals who are truant or who set fires but who do not meet criteria for Conduct Disorder will elaborate the nature of the problem in a different way.

To researchers working in the field, the study of subtypes of conduct disorder may address the recommendations. For example, in the study of conduct disorder, the current efforts to identify subtypes are a move toward greater specificity. A line of work suggests that conduct disorder may have a child onset or adolescent onset and that youths differ considerably depending on this pattern. The present recommendations are not for replacing this line of work but to supplement it with more specific lines of work. Child or adolescent onset continues the global, broad groupings. Finer grained analyses ought to supplement these broad foci in the study of conduct problems.

An advantage to seeking increased specificity in the focus on behavioral problems is to permit the development of mini-theories about a problem area. A mini-theory accounts for specific facets of conduct disorder rather than attempting a comprehensive explanation of how the full range of dysfunctions has emerged. For example, Patterson (1982) has developed coercion theory to explain the development of aggressive behavior in the homes of antisocial youths. The theory does not really explain stealing, setting fires, truancy, and other aspects of conduct disorder. However, the processes leading to aggression have been examined empirically in sophisticated ways. Even within the context of aggressive behavior, the theory might be criticized for leaving many questions unanswered (e.g., why a particular child becomes aggressive rather than a sibling) or for neglecting to incorporate important influences on aggressive behavior (e.g., genetic contributions, TV violence). Yet such criticism fails to acknowledge the remarkable research that this model has spawned (see Patterson et al., 1992). The limited focus of the theory has aided rather than hindered conceptualization of the entire range of antisocial behaviors by uncovering subgroups (e.g., aggressors, stealers) for whom specific processes are less applicable. Although not as well developed or tested, mini-theories have emerged to explain truancy (Galloway, 1985) and firesetting (Kolko & Kazdin, 1986). Such efforts raise hopes for finer grained analyses of these subgroups of antisocial children.

Although advances in diagnosis continue to emerge seeking to understand conduct disorder and antisocial behavior at a more general level, research on more focused problem areas is essential as well. The increased need for specificity in studying antisocial behavior does not compete with goals of diagnosis. Nor does the focus on samples with specific types of problems deny the established findings that conduct problem symptoms tend to go together. Studying more specific patterns or key symptoms may permit better ways of organizing or grouping youth and supplement existing work on the broader diagnostic category.

Extension of Diagnosis

Diagnosis refers to identification of problems or symptoms of the child. The notion and use of diagnosis has derived from the study of medical illness in relation to identifying a disease based on the symptoms. In relation to conduct disorder, it would be useful to consider diagnosis in a broader context. Many other domains are important for identifying the paths leading to the disorder, the various responses to treatments, and the long-term course of the disorder. For example, characteristics of a child other than symptoms (e.g., prosocial functioning, intelligence levels) are known to relate to clinical course and long-term adjustment, as discussed earlier in the book. In addition, other domains are relevant that relate to contexts in which conduct disorder emerges.

To convey the point, consider two youths who are virtually identical in their sets and severity levels of conduct disorder symptoms. However, one youth comes from a family with a history of conduct disorder, lives with a single parent who abuses drugs, and is involved in a network of delinquent peers. The other child comes from a family without a history of psychiatric impairment or criminal activity, and is doing well academically at school. We could say that these children both meet criteria for the disorder but differ greatly on extenuating circumstances and associated features. Yet this is of little help in understanding the systematic differences in domains such as the family either for research or clinical work. What is needed is the development of ways of assessing and categorizing contexts so they can be studied more systematically.

An expanded diagnostic scheme would evaluate youths along several domains. For example, individuals can be assessed on a variety of domains such as parent and family functioning, peer relations, and neighborhoods. From the information, one might construct profiles of each case across multiple domains of their lives. A *profile* refers to systematic assessment of several dimensions and the display of the individuals scores across these dimensions. Each individual can be scored on each dimension separately; patterns or configurations of dimensions can be studied as well.

The notion of a profile of functioning is already familiar. Profile types have been very well developed and studied in the context of standardized assessment techniques (e.g., as in research on the Minnesota Multiphasic Personality Inventory [MMPI-2]; Graham, 1990). In child assessment, the development and standardization of versions of the Child Behavior Checklist (e.g., Achenbach, 1991) provide information about diverse domains of child dysfunction. From these profiles, one can examine patterns of characteristics, rather than only the scores of particular characteristics. The pattern allows for the construction of empirically based typologies that can then be studied in their own right. Research would benefit from a profile of the child's life in ways that cover multiple characteristics of child, parent, family, and contexts. With a broader profile, we can begin to describe the matrices in which children develop. We can then begin to use these matrices as a way of developing models of treatment and testing models.

Current assessment of child dysfunction, whether through diagnostic instruments or parent, teacher, and child rating scales adhere to a descriptive, phenomenological approach. The goal is to describe the scope of dysfunction. Behind the approach is the assumption that child *dysfunction* ought to be the main or sole assessment focus. Our understanding of conduct disorder would profit from a broader conceptualization of the settings and context in which child functioning are embedded. These settings and contexts, at present, cannot be systematically assessed and investigated very well. Systems are needed to permit "diagnosis," categorization, and dimensionalization of these other domains for their investigation. Development of systematic assessments of broader domains is needed to permit their evaluation. Profile types involving patterns of characteristics that go together in relation to child, parent, family, and context will provide opportunities for new levels of understanding the disorder.

General Comments

The previous comments refer to finer grained levels of analyses at two levels. The first level pertains to the study of individual problem domains. It is important to ask questions about conduct disorder—such as, who "has" the disorder, how did they arrive at that point, and what are the many characteristics (parent, family) associated with that. The same questions might well be asked of samples identified more narrowly: for example, who sets fires, how did they arrive at that point? The samples that are identified by key problems (e.g., fighting, stealing, lying) no doubt will have other symptoms than those used for their selection. Yet the yield of information is likely to be quite different from that derived from the broadly defined conduct disorder group.

The second level pertains to the systematic study of a broad range of characteristics in which conduct disorder is embedded. We have ways of "typing" disorders and individuals, but no such ways of typing family contexts, neighborhoods, peer groups, and so on. Assessment of the child across a range of domains in systematic ways is needed as the basis to study more complex relations among problems of the child and their relations to other domains.

SAMPLING ISSUES

Sampling has many meanings but is often raised in the context of selecting cases for inclusion in a study. The topic is raised here because the samples of youth chosen for investigation, the neglect of subsamples, and the sampling of risk factors can greatly limit our understanding of conduct disorder.

Spectrum of Dysfunction

The samples of youths with conduct disorder included in research warrant expansion both for purposes of understanding the nature and development of the problems as well as for intervention. There are several separate issues here that convey the importance of expanding the samples that we study. In current research, there is a point at which a youth is considered to be sufficiently dysfunctional to meet criteria for

Conduct Disorder or to be delineated in some other way (e.g., delin-quent). A significant issue pertains to the threshold for making the di-agnosis or designation. In current diagnosis (*DSM-IV*), as an illus-tration, the presence of at least three symptoms for at least 12 months is required to meet the criteria for disorder. In principle, it is superb to specify criteria in this fashion so that diagnoses can be reliably made and that research on these samples can be replicated. Yet the criteria themselves are not very defensible. Where one draws the cutoff point to decide dysfunction (e.g., three symptoms rather than four or eight; duration of 12 months rather than 18, 24, or more) is likely to lead to different findings with regard to risk and protective factors, responsive-ness to treatment, prognosis, and so on.

The criteria for deciding the presence versus absence of disorder can-not be viewed as having a strong justification. Clearly, youths who do meet the criteria are likely to be significantly impaired and that is im-portant to know for all sorts of reasons (e.g., making referrals to treat-ment, providing reimbursement for services). Yet for understanding the nature of conduct disorder more generally, it is important to extend re-search to the full spectrum of severity of impairment and dysfunction. For example, fighting, if of interest as a dysfunction, might be studied across the full spectrum of youths within a given age range, rather than only at the level of severity and frequency meeting the criteria for the designation of Conduct Disorder. Alternatively, youths who show the symptoms of Conduct Disorder but who are at, above, or below the diagnosis threshold (e.g., have fewer than three symptoms, three to four symptoms, or more than four symptoms, respectively, as one way to operationalize threshold) would be important to study. The advantage of studying the broad spectrum is to permit evaluation of factors that predict functioning across the spectrum of severity and frequency as well as those that just predict at different points (e.g., among only those youths who fight often, or with peers and adults).

A second, perhaps more important, advantage to studying the full spectrum of functioning is to decide where the cutoff point ought to be. Conduct disorder and nonconduct disorder youths represent extremes. The category "conduct disorder" is "fuzzy" insofar as some individuals are at each extreme (clearly conduct disorder, or clearly not); however, there are many shades in the middle (see Kazdin & Kagan, 1994). In-vestigation of the spectrum of severity of conduct disorder or severity of a particular type of problem domain is important to help establish meaningful cutoff points. Presumably, there are points on the continuum that identify clinical features such as a particularly poor prognosis or the failure to respond to treatment. The full spectrum warrants much more attention to understand where the points are warranted to be delineated for intervention.

Sampling Across Case Characteristics

Studies of conduct disorder often are restricted to selected samples that may limit the findings. From the standpoint of research design, the investigators often seek homogeneous samples and hence do not select diverse individuals. The reason is to reduce sources of variability (error) that may obscure relations that are under investigation. The general research practice per se is not being questioned. Rather much of the conduct disorder research has systematically restricted samples in ways that are likely to alter our conclusions about conduct disorder and its onset, characteristics, and outcome. Two restrictions in particular warrant comment.

First, there is a "sex bias" in the study of conduct disorder. A number of research programs focus exclusively on boys. Of course, this focus has an empirical rationale given much higher rates of the disorder among boys than girls. The higher rates make males easier to study (e.g., to recruit cases, to identify other characteristics in which the base rate of an outcome might be low). Yet the tendency to ignore girls and young women in research on conduct disorder and the failure to study both sexes limit our understanding of conduct disorder. We already know important differences from the instances in which sex differences have been evaluated. For example, boys and girls, whether in community or clinic samples, vary in the extent to which they are perpetrators or victims of aggression and in the constellation of factors in early development that predict onset and long-term course of aggressive and antisocial behavior (e.g., Eron et al., 1991; Olweus, 1991; Tremblay et al., 1992). If the factors that influence onset of antisocial behavior vary for male and female youths, then effective preventive and treatment interventions may vary as well.

Of course, we do not merely want to study girls more frequently, but rather to make sure that both sexes are included in the same study. The reason is to ensure that youths are studied in the same way, using the same measures and predictors and the same cohort. Sex differences are more readily interpreted within a given study rather than between studies when all sorts of differences in procedures, measures, and other factors of the evaluation are allowed to vary.

Ethnic and racial differences also are important evaluate in relation to dysfunction. Ethnic group differences are also likely to vary greatly in the factors that contribute to risk and protection. Important differences exist among European American, African American, and Hispanic American children in prevalence, age of onset, course, and specific risk factors related to dysfunction. For example, among those suffering from substance abuse, ethnicity correlates with the specific substance used, the degree of family monitoring, risk factors, and amount of exposure (Catalano et al., 1993; Maddahian, Newcomb, & Bentler, 1988). Occasionally, interventions designed to prevent conduct disorder vary in their effectiveness as a function of ethnic group. For example, one prevention program (Hawkins et al., 1991) found intervention effects for Caucasian but not for African American youths. The basis of these differences are by no means clear.

Sex and ethnic differences are not the only variables to consider. Yet these two are important and serve as a basis for articulating the problem we wish to avoid. Research is often interested in developing models or theories of dysfunction and then proceeding to test these with very restricted samples. If the model is intended to be applicable only to a particular sex or race, the sample meets the goals of the research. Yet researchers usually discuss their conceptual models more broadly as if they explain conduct disorder in general. Sex and ethnicity are good candidates for variables that moderate several influences and hence warrant much greater attention. We know this not from armchair reflection about sex and ethnic differences but rather from isolated findings that these variables do make a difference when they are specifically studied.

Spectrum of Risk Factors

Sampling issues emerge in yet another way. Researchers are interested in studying variables that influence child functioning. In psychological research, for example, this is often accomplished by studies in which groups are selected and compared based on their exposure to (or experience of) an event. For example, the effects of abusive child-rearing practices on children and adolescents are often studied in this way. In some research, one identifies abused and nonabused children and identifies other characteristics they might show (e.g., symptoms of psychopathology, school performance, peer relations). There are several separate sampling issues here. First, it is important to sample separately or multiple points across a given risk factor. Identification of extreme groups is an excellent point of departure for beginning work in an area. But we wish to understand the continuum of the characteristic. In the case of discipline practices, we wish to know how these affect children in general and the point at which these practices become risk factors.[1]

Studying multiple levels of a proposed risk factor is important to reveal the function (or relation) in a more finely grained fashion than the study of two groups (e.g., having the presence or absence of a particular characteristic). Many influences are likely to bear curvilinear relations to an outcome of interest; the assessment of different levels of the risk characteristic can reveal this. For example, the degree to which parents try to control their adolescents is related to externalizing symptoms and drug use (Stice, Barrera, & Chassin, 1993). However, the relation is not linear. Extremely high or low parental control, but not intermediate control, is associated with adolescent dysfunction. Similarly, adolescent alcohol use is correlated with current dysfunction and lack of academic pursuits, job instability, and disorganized thought processes years later (McGee & Newcomb, 1992; Newcomb & Bentler, 1988). Yet the relation of alcohol use either to current or later consequences is not linear. Heavy alcohol use predicts later problems; no alcohol use or consumption whatsoever is associated with undesirable personal and social characteristics as well. Those with the best level of adjustment used a small amount of alcohol; this was associated with several positive outcomes including decreased loneliness, reduced self-derogation, improved relationships with family and others, and increased social support. The point of these examples is to convey the need to study multiple levels of factors presumed (or indeed known) to increase risk for dysfunction. There may be points at which a given factor has one effect (risk), another at which it has no effect, or another level at which it may even have a protective effect for an outcome of interest.

Second and related, risk factors are likely to interact with each other and with third variables. It is not as if abuse, whenever it occurs, will have a particular effect. Rather the deleterious effects may depend on other factors (e.g., child temperament, marital conflict, child IQ). A finer grained understanding of a particular risk factor of interest can be obtained by evaluating levels of that factor in relation to another factor as well. For example, we know that large family size is a risk factor for conduct disorder. However, sampling across families of different incomes reveals a more fine grained understanding of large family size. This is a risk factor for families with a low income; families with sufficient funds to support a large family are not at risk.

General Comments

Much is known about conduct disorder and this has come from quite different studies using varying definitions of the problem, quite different populations (e.g., delinquents), and youths of different ages. That consistencies have emerged across many studies attests to the robustness of the problems. At the same time, further understanding may be limited without consideration of different samples and moderators of the findings. Sex and ethnic group are among two of the moderators. Also, finer grained study of risk characteristics and the extent to which they are moderated by other factors will be important as well.

EXPANDING THE MODELS TO DEVELOP AND TO EVALUATE INTERVENTIONS

There have been clear advances in the areas of both treatment and prevention. Empirically based interventions can be identified that have had direct impact on the problem. Even so, the ways in which interventions are studied and delivered may greatly limit their effectiveness. New models of implementing and evaluating interventions are needed.

In the usual model of intervention research, whether treatment or prevention, a specific intervention is applied to an identified sample (e.g., clinically referred or at risk youths) for a specific, time-limited duration; after the intervention is terminated its effects are then evaluated. Consider these characteristics as representing a *conventional model* of implementing and evaluating interventions. The limits of the model are especially evident in treatment studies, in which the interventions are often quite brief (e.g., 8 to 10 weeks). In prevention studies, interventions often are implemented over a period of a few years. Even so, the comments about the limits of the conventional model apply, in varying degrees, to both treatment and prevention. Making explicit the main characteristics of conventional intervention research helps us to describe alternative models to guide research.

High-Strength Intervention Model

In the conventional model, treatment obviously is intended to have impact but rarely is it explicitly designed to provide a particularly potent test. In contrast, the high-strength intervention model begins with an effort to maximize therapeutic change. For severe clinical problems in particular, it may be valuable to address the question, "What is the likely impact on the problem with the maximum or seemingly most potent treatment(s) available?" One should aim for the *strongest feasible version* of treatment to see if the problem can be altered. The high-strength model is an effort not only to maximize clinical change, but also to test the limits (or strengths) of our knowledge at a given point. Given the best available treatment(s), what can we expect from the maximum dose, regimen, or variation?

For psychosocial treatments, strength and intensity of treatment are difficult to define. The problem stems in part from nebulous or poor conceptualizations of treatment. To vary or increase the strength of treatment, one must have some idea regarding the procedures or processes that account for therapeutic change. To convey the possible change that the high-strength model of treatment reflects relative to the conventional model, consider one parameter of treatment—namely, duration of therapy. In contemporary child and adolescent therapy research, the mean duration of treatment is between 8 and 10 weeks (Casey & Berman, 1985; Kazdin, Bass et al., 1990). This duration is relatively brief considering the many problems that conduct disorder children bring to treatment and their poor long-term prognosis. More (treatment) is not invariably better. At the same time, current tests by and large seem weak. Much longer treatments, perhaps even spanning years, might seem more promising at maximizing impact. Again, duration is a single parameter of treatment mentioned here merely to illustrate the model; it is not one of the salient dimensions or characteristics on which high-strength treatments necessarily depend.

High-strength interventions may be costly, as reflected in the expense of therapists, therapist training, number of sessions, and patient contact hours. Yet even if such a test were very expensive in terms of professional resources and patient care, the resulting knowledge might obviate the need for multiple other tests with weaker versions of treatment. If the strongest version of treatment produces change, then it is reasonable to study whether less protracted, less costly, and less difficult to implement procedures can achieve similar outcomes. It is also reasonable to study whether any loss in treatment gains is worth the savings in cost or ease of administration. However, knowledge of what can be accomplished is important for both a test of current knowledge and for clinical care.

A critical limitation to applying high-strength treatment is what consumers (i.e., children, parents, third-party payers) will allow. The idea of protracted and intensive treatment for deviant behavior is not as familiar, or, probably, as well accepted as is protracted punishment for criminal acts. Also, with current treatments, it is often difficult to retain cases because of the high dropout rates. Yet such practical problems are surmountable. For example, patients could be paid for coming to and participating in treatment—not necessarily an expensive alternative if the costs of untreated conduct disorder are considered. No doubt other strategies for retaining cases can be pursued as well. In addition, stronger treatments do not necessarily translate into longer sessions and more sessions for reasons noted previously. Additional research is needed aiming at effecting change with stronger treatments than have been tested. Such evaluations would provide improved tests of the extent to which current treatments can effectively alter severe conduct disorder.

Amenability-to-Treatment Model

Implicit in much of intervention research is the view that the specific technique, at the exclusion of other factors, accounts for most of the change (or variance) that is achieved. This view can be inferred by the almost exclusive focus on treatment and treatment variations as the basis for treatment outcome studies (Kazdin, Bass et al., 1990). The amenability-to-treatment model considers child, parent, and family factors that might moderate the effects of treatment. The model is designed to identify which interventions are likely to be successful—namely, with those children who are most *amenable to treatment.* Conduct disorder youths represent a heterogeneous group in terms of dysfunction(s), adaptive skills, and resources (e.g., family support). There are remarkable leads from research on risk and protective factors related to child, parent, family, and to contexts that might be used to identify youths likely to vary in their amenability to change. For example, children with early onset of antisocial behavior and who engage in diverse behaviors across multiple settings (e.g., home and school) are more likely to continue antisocial behavior into adolescence and adulthood. Age of onset and several other child, parent, and family characteristics can be distinguished among youths who are referred clinically for conduct disorder; these variables may influence amenability or responsiveness to treatment.

The amenability model considers the population of conduct disorder youths as varying in degrees of amenability to treatment. Where to begin is not necessarily fixed in the model. One obvious point would begin with evaluating, in a systematic way, the impact of treatment on those youths who should be the most amenable to treatment. We know from follow-up studies that parent psychopathology, marital conflict, stress, and socioeconomic disadvantage seem to predict minimal response to treatment, as discussed earlier. Using these variables, can we identify a subgroup of youths who, when treated, tend to respond rather well, that is, with potent and durable change? Progress in treatment might be accelerated by selecting the subgroups that can be effectively treated. Testing of amenable cases does not mean neglect of the more recalcitrant cases. However, in the accumulation of knowledge, ways of dividing the population so as to treat any subgroup effectively would be a major accomplishment. Also, once subgroups of youths who can be effectively treated are identified, a more concentrated focus can be provided to those less amenable and for whom effective treatments are unavailable.

Few studies have systematically explored the differential amenability of children to treatment. For example, in one study, institutionalized delinquents ($N = 400$, age range = 17 to 23 years) were randomly assigned to treatment (i.e., counseling, group therapy) or to a nontreatment control group (Adams, 1970). Treated youths who were judged as "amenable" (i.e., more intelligent, verbal, anxious, insightful, aware of their problems, and interested in change) showed significantly less recidivism than controls. In contrast, nonamenable treated youths did worse in comparison to controls. The study points to the potential benefits of delineating youths by their likely amenability to treatment in predicting differential treatment outcomes.

The approach of identifying youths more or less amenable to treatment can be integrated into existing controlled outcome research. Within a given study, youths can be identified as more or less amenable to the intervention based on characteristics of the sample and hypotheses about the interface of treatment and these characteristics. Analyses of outcome effects are then based on comparisons of subgroups within the investigation to assess responsiveness to treatment as a function of hypothesized amenability to treatment.

Broad-Based Interventions

Conduct disorder is multifaceted; it includes a broad range of symptoms, areas of dysfunction, and parent and family problems. For many, if not most diagnosable cases, conduct disorder represents a "pervasive developmental disorder" in the sense that broad areas of functioning are deleteriously affected. In conventional applications of treatment, a particular intervention is implemented to alter an important facet (e.g., psychic conflict, self-esteem, family processes) of the child, or of the system in which the child functions, or of both. For example, individual therapy with the child might focus on the child's expression of anger or unresolved conflict. Parent management training might focus on child-rearing practices as a way to alter conduct disorder. In these and many other treatments, a particular conceptual model emphasizes a domain—usually one domain that is considered to be central to the child's problem. In light of the range of deficits and pervasiveness of the dysfunction that conduct disorder represents, the focus of most treatments may be quite narrow.

The broad-based intervention model is an effort to expand the comprehensiveness or scope of interventions to address a large set of domains relevant to the individual youth's dysfunction. Treatments can be conceived in a *modular fashion* in which there are separate components (or modules) woven into an overall treatment regimen. Implementation of the model requires separate steps. The model begins with evaluation of child functioning in diverse domains (e.g., home, school, community, deviance, interpersonal behavior, academic functioning). Then treatment provides multiple approaches designed to address the domains of functioning identified as problematic. Plausible treatment combinations might include individual psychotherapy or cognitively based treatment, school-based reinforcement, family therapy, and parent training. As a preview to later comments, in clinical practice, therapists often say they do just this—namely, identify domains of dysfunction and then provide treatment to address these. The very unsystematic, idiosyncratic, and unevaluated way this is done is not the model advocated here.

Occasionally, multiple treatments are combined in modular fashion in research to redress multiple domains of dysfunction. For example, Satterfield and his colleagues (Satterfield, Satterfield, & Schell, 1987) evaluated the short- and long-term impact of treatment on hyperactive children (ages 6 to 12). Treatment with medication alone was compared to a multimodal treatment that included medication and several other approaches (e.g., individual psychotherapy, group therapy, parent and family therapy, educational therapy, and cognitive-behavior modification in the home). The treatments varied, based on an ongoing evaluation of what each case was judged to need by the treatment team. Follow-up results, approximately 9 years after treatment, showed significantly lower rates of arrests for felony offences and of institutionalization for the multimodal children compared to the medication-only children. The benefits of multimodal therapy are suggested by this study. Unfortunately, the decision rules for providing the individual modules were not specified; hence replication in research and practice may be difficult.

Other examples can be provided in which multiple modalities of treatment were combined based on evaluating the individual case and domains of dysfunction. Already mentioned in the review of treatments was multisystemic therapy, which uses a variety of treatments for the individual child, parent, and family (e.g., problem-solving skills training, parent management training, marital therapy, and a variety of individualized programs to alter problem domains such as peer relations). Here, too, the guidelines for deciding when to provide which treatments, in what amounts, and for which youths and families warrant greater specification. Even so, the investigation of multifaceted treatments designed to address several domains of dysfunction is a major advance.

The idea of broad-based and multifaceted treatments is not an endorsement for eclecticism in treatment in which multiple interventions are used to meet the putative "individual needs of the client." Rarely are the putative needs known, systematically assessed, or used as a basis for selecting among the very diverse psychotherapies and medications available for treatment. Also, the agglomeration of techniques is often haphazard with multiple procedures being selected for their intuitive appeal and face validity or mandates (e.g., accreditation requirements) not based on theory or research. In the broad-based model, the combination is justified on the basis of the assessment of specific domains prior to treatment and an effort to match dysfunction in these domains to alternative interventions based on conceptualization or evidence in behalf of these interventions.

In general, the purpose of combining interventions is to address different facets of the problem of antisocial behavior. The combination is justified on the basis of evidence that different domains are relevant to and predict future antisocial behavior *and* on the basis of the absence of clearly defined individual treatments at present that reliably ameliorate conduct disorder or controvert its long-term course. The combination of interventions requires careful consideration and conceptual justification to avoid the mere collection of techniques, each of which might be administered in a well-intentioned but highly diluted fashion. Many current treatments suffer from weak conceptual bases already. The combination of multiple techniques without regard to what they are supposed to accomplish and how they are to be administered potentially compounds the problem.

Future research might move toward a more comprehensive approach with multiple interventions. The approach should be guided by initial evidence that the constituent techniques produce some change and that the domain of the focus is relevant to the problem. Promising applications of this model are in place already. For example, one prevention program currently underway applies several previously studied interventions (i.e., parent management training, social skills training, academic tutoring, and classroom intervention) to prevent conduct disorder (Conduct Problems Prevention Research Group, 1992).[2] Of course, a concern when multifaceted treatments are studied is that at the end of the investigation one cannot identify which component(s) accounted for change. Yet once such a multifaceted treatment is shown to produce change, it might then be quite worthwhile to begin to analyze the contributions of individual components.

A Chronic-Care Model

The conventional model of treatment focuses on brief intervention. Implicit in this view is that the problem can be ameliorated with a restricted and time-limited intervention. The analogy in medicine might be treating infection with an antibiotic for a regimen of, say, 10 days. For many infections, a brief, time-limited intervention is effective. Yet perhaps a different model ought to guide our thinking about treatments for conduct disorder. Chronic disease, for example, by its nature requires long-term care. There are, of course, many chronic diseases; here, too, one might distinguish different models of providing treatment based on their varied characteristics, underlying causes, and the responses they elicit. Among many diseases, diabetes is relatively familiar and one that illustrates the issues that are applicable to conduct disorder. Diabetes mellitus is a disease with multiple manifestations and variations. Stated oversimply, the disease consists of the insufficient production of insulin. Characteristically, diabetes is viewed as a chronic condition. Treatment is based on the assumption that the person suffers from a condition that requires continued care, management, and treatment. An effective treatment (e.g., insulin) for a delimited period would not, after termination, be expected to ameliorate the problem.

Research on conduct disorder suggests that it is very much like a chronic condition in terms of its development and course. Also, the dysfunction has broad impact both during childhood and adolescence (e.g., in affecting behavior at home and at school; interpersonal, academic, and cognitive spheres) and during adulthood (e.g., psychological, social, and work adjustment). It might be heuristically valuable to consider conduct disorder as a chronic condition that requires intervention, continued monitoring, and evaluation over the course of one's life.

Perhaps after a child is referred, treatment is provided, either in the usual way (conventional model) or based on other models (e.g., high-strength intervention, broad-based intervention) noted previously. In the chronic care-approach, after improvement is achieved, treatment is suspended rather than terminated. At that point, the child or adolescent begins to be monitored systematically (i.e., with standardized measures) and regularly (e.g., every 3 months). Treatment could be provided *pro re nata* (PRN) based on the assessment data or on emergent issues raised by the family, teachers, or others. The model of treatment and monitoring might be likened to the more familiar model of dental care in the United States in which individuals are checked every 6 months; an intervention is provided if and as needed based on these periodic checks.

A related but alternative model would be to continue therapy beyond the initial treatment period. Initial treatment would redress the crises and problematic functioning. Instead of termination and regular monitoring alone, children could enter into maintenance therapy, that is, continued treatment perhaps in varying schedules ("doses"). Essentially cases are continued in treatment but on a less intensive basis. The model has been effective in treating recurrent depression in adults (see Kupfer et al., 1992).

Obviously, the use of ongoing treatment is not advocated in cases in which there is evidence that short-term treatment is effective. Indeed, short-term treatment is compatible with a more chronic treatment regimen. The model requires monitoring children who are likely to continue dysfunction so that treatment can be reintroduced as needed. This is a very different conceptualization of what is needed for treatment. Under current financial pressures in health care, the move is invariably toward less care and less treatment. Research designed to test alternative interventions often reflects this pressure, and, in that way, contribute to its continuation. There is no reason to believe that conduct disorder requires brief treatment and much evidence that would lead one to expect otherwise.

What precisely is gained by adopting a chronic-care model? Actually a great deal. The conventional model has not established that a brief time-limited treatment can control conduct disorder. However, several cognitive, behavioral, family, and community-based interventions, beyond the promising treatments highlighted earlier, have shown that they can effect change (see Kazdin, 1985). Follow-up data are unavailable for most treatment studies. For some treatments, follow-up has indicated that benefits are lost when treatment is terminated. However, with the chronic-care model, the shorter term changes are quite respectable because treatment is continued on an as needed basis. Intermittent continuation of treatment would be reasonable until more abbreviated treatments with long-term impact are identified.

General Comments

Typically, intervention research on conduct disorder is conducted in ways opposite from what might be needed to develop and to identify effective interventions. Treatment research illustrates these deficiencies (Kazdin, Bass et al., 1990). For example, in treatment research, the amount and duration of treatment is relatively brief (e.g., 1 hour sessions, 8 to 10 sessions total), probably not a sufficient test of a high-strength treatment. Child, parent, family, and other characteristics are rarely examined to identify who is more or less amenable or responsive to treatment. Individual techniques are usually contrasted with one another, rather than combined in an effort to augment therapeutic change.

Thus broad-based treatments are not usually tested. Finally, the brevity of treatment, already mentioned, and the lack of continued monitoring as a basis to bring people back into treatment conveys the absence of the chronic-care model. These characteristics of therapy research would not be problematic if effective treatments were identified with the conventional model of treatment evaluation. However, the yield from research and the very severe and pervasive impairment of many conduct disorder youths serve as impetus to reconsider the focus, design, and model of treatment trials.

Prevention research has been more likely to adopt facets of the previously discussed models. Usually interventions are longer (e.g., often 1 to 3 years) and are broad based (e.g., focusing on child, parent, and family functioning; adaptive behavior of the child; and preacademic performance). Prevention research often begins with consideration of multiple risk factors and hence has a broad focus. Even so, prevention research omits several features of the models discussed previously that could advance the field. Rarely is there an effort to identify and to predict who will be more amenable to treatment. Also, interventions may need to be much longer than the time-limited ones included in prevention studies.

The models advocated here might be cast aside as impractical. For example, the chronic-care model as a guide to treatment or prevention may seem quite unfeasible. There are already facets of "mental health" problems that are viewed as similar to a chronic condition (e.g., the Alcoholics Anonymous treatment model). It is likely that clinical depression will be seen more in this light as well. Even though major depression is episodic (e.g., waxes and wanes), this pattern itself is chronic for many individuals. Conduct disorder reflects a chronic and more stable condition for many individuals. Perhaps providing ongoing and chronic treatment is not the most crucial feature. The critical feature is to assess the youth's progress periodically (e.g., at home, school, and the community) to monitor the extent to which he or she is adjusting well, and to use the information to reapply treatment. Indeed, the key to treating diabetes has been the assessment of the extent to which the patient has control over blood glucose levels. Whether treatment is to be increased, decreased, or altered markedly depends on the feedback that assessment provides. Assessment of a child's or adolescent's progress does not raise insurmountable problems for the application of a similar model.

SOCIAL POLICY AND ACTION

Drawing on Knowledge for Intervention

From a scientific standpoint, many questions remain regarding conduct disorder. Many of these questions are rather fundamental, including what are the best ways of delineating (i.e., diagnosing, categorizing) conduct disorder, how do risk and protective factors operate, and for whom can the path toward conduct disorder be interrupted or altered completely? Also, by the very nature of how theory and research operate, many findings that seem solid are open for debate or subject to tremendous qualification. The simple statements that one would like to derive from scientific findings often depart from the findings themselves. So, for example, for clarity's sake, it would be great if we could state simply that poverty, physical abuse of the child, parent psychopathology, poor peer relations, or, even better, all these and other risk factors beginning with p lead to conduct disorder. This kind of simplicity is not permitted by the nature of what is known.

At this same time, a great deal is known or at least partially known and this can provide a reasonable basis for action that can have social impact. This is not a matter of looking at the glass (the knowledge base) as half empty or half full. Often imperfect knowledge is sufficient to have impact and to make progress. For example, the nature of memory processes is being elaborated at the neurobiological level, and the complete picture of how memories are stored, retrieved, and altered at that level is far from resolved. At the same time, enough is known at a different level to help people store, retain, and retrieve information better (e.g., type of practice, use of cognitive schemes for coding material). Roughly analogously, much can be done to reduce conduct disorder in individuals and society at large, even while the puzzles of its origins and processes are being put together.

Expert panels from various professions as well as from government agencies have convened with the purpose of sifting through the knowledge base and providing recommendations. For example, a Commission on Violence and Youth of the American Psychological Association (1993) provided a 2-year study (and a 2-volume report) and concluded that, "society can intervene effectively in the lives of children and youth to reduce or prevent their involvement in violence" (p. 5). Several specific suggestions were elaborated to convey how this can be

TABLE 6.1 Overview of Recommendations to Curb Violence

- Early childhood interventions directed toward parents, childcare providers, and healthcare providers to help build the critical foundation of attitudes, knowledge, and behavior related to aggression.
- School-based interventions to help schools provide safe environments and effective programs to prevent violence.
- Heightened awareness of cultural diversity and involvement of members of the community in planning, implementing, and evaluating intervention efforts.
- Development of the mass media's potential to be part of the solution to violence, not just a contributor to the problem.
- Limiting access to firearms by children and youths and teaching them how to prevent firearm violence.
- Reduction of youth involvement with alcohol and other drugs (known to be contributing factors to violence by youths) and to family violence directed at youths.
- Psychological health services for young perpetrators, victims, and witnesses to violence in order to avert the trajectory toward later involvement in more serious violence.
- Education programs to reduce prejudice and hostility (factors leading to hate crimes and violence against social groups).
- Efforts to strengthen the ability of police and community leaders to prevent mob violence by early and appropriate intervention.
- Efforts by psychologists acting as individuals and through professional organizations to reduce violence among youths.

SOURCE: The Executive Summary of the Report of the American Psychological Association Commission on Violence and Youth. (1993). *Violence and youth: Psychology's response* (Vol. 1). Copyright 1993 by the American Psychological Association. Reprinted by permission.

accomplished. Table 6.1 summarizes the categories of actions that can be taken. Each of these categories was developed in detail to convey their connection to what is known from current research on risk factors, onset of dysfunction, and interventions.

Prevention of conduct disorder, and indeed of dysfunctions among children, adolescents, and adults, has received special attention in relation to recommendations for action. For example, a panel of experts from the Institute of Medicine of the National Academy of Sciences (i.e., the Committee on Prevention of Mental Disorders) reviewed the current status of research on mental illness and problem behaviors and on the promotion of mental health to provide recommendations on policies and programs (Mrazek & Haggerty, 1994). As another example, the National Institute of Mental Health, a central source of funding of research on prevention of mental illness and promotion of mental health, provided a comprehensive review of their own scientific activities and issued a report that outlined progress in the field, objectives of current work, and future needs to continue and to accelerate progress (Reiss, 1993).

In general, these latter reports focus on what can be accomplished to improve society; even more attention has been given to what is needed to develop the knowledge base and to apply what is known. In this regard, the reports emphasize the importance of improving governmental infrastructure to support preventive efforts (e.g., coordination of efforts by different agencies, centralization of prevention efforts with new agencies), the need to increase training opportunities for professionals so that a sufficient number of scientists and research centers can provide the needed training opportunities, the requirements for improvements in research and demonstration projects to prevent various problems such as conduct disorder. The recommendations in these reports and others that may be cited emphasize the need for basic research on the underpinnings of adjustment and maladjustment. Many diverse disciplines participate in this research, including the social, behavioral, biological, and health sciences—including, but not limited to, the fields of criminology, epidemiology, genetics, neuroscience, psychology, psychiatry, nursing, and social work.

Commissions, reports, and recommendations are available in large numbers. Recommendations and reports often are not translated into action in large part because of the very many social issues that warrant intervention and the need to prioritize which among them are to receive attention. Also, commission reports often conclude, correctly, that efforts related to the area under study will require more resources, money, agencies, training programs, and so on. Analyses of what is needed to make progress (proposed funds) are matched against the costs of the problem and often reveal that up-front money now will eventually prove to be less expensive in the long run. Even when this case is persuasively made, this does not always mean that funds are available now for investing in the more long-term solution.

Prevention, Treatment, and Social Responsibility

Recommendations for ameliorating conduct disorder emphasize prevention, based on advances in that area. From a policy as well as research perspective, prevention and treatment often are juxtaposed in a competitive fashion in which one is proposed as the better way to address conduct disorder (e.g., aggressive and antisocial behavior). The costs of treatment, the greater difficulty to treat more severe impairment, and limited professional resources to deliver treatment are advanced as central reasons to emphasize early preventive interventions.

From the standpoint of reducing conduct disorder, there is little point in justifying one focus (e.g., treatment or prevention) at the expense of the other. The limited funding resources contribute to the polarization of prevention and treatment. The resource constraints themselves need to be reconsidered. Also, neither prevention nor treatment, nor one type of approach or intervention within these domains (e.g., primary prevention, social competence promotion) can be expected to single-handedly resolve aggression and antisocial behaviors among children. For example, it is unlikely that primary prevention will be unequivocally successful across the full range of at-risk behaviors and conditions that contribute to aggression so as to obviate treatment. Few proponents of prevention would suggest this is a reasonable expectation. As noted in the previous chapter, within even very high quality programs, there is often considerable variability in how well, or how consistently, the intervention is implemented, and in the degree of impact it has on the youths. Among those youths for whom the intervention is well implemented and effective, there are still many who engage in conduct problem behaviors, even though these may be at a lower rate than is seen among youths in the nonintervention group. In principle, as well as practice, there are limits on the impact of prevention. This is not an argument against prevention, but rather serves to convey that many additional efforts are required for prevention to have a significant impact.

Diverse intervention efforts and a broad portfolio of approaches are central to reducing conduct disorder in childhood and adolescence. As a beginning, large-scale programs for maternal care and child intervention directed to early risk factors for poor adjustment (e.g., involving maternal nutrition, baby care, child-rearing and early education) can have broad effects on mothers and their offspring for a extended period (Zigler et al., 1992). The focus of such programs is on packages of risk factors that are known to have adverse effects. Large-scale universal programs for children and adolescents in the schools are also important to promote positive social competence and resistance to internal and peer pressures that might lead to antisocial behavior. Universal programs do not necessarily replace more focused or targeted interventions for youths who are at high risk or who show early signs of antisocial behavior. The task is to identify a range of interventions, settings in which they can be deployed, ages at which they are maximally effective, and so on. In this process, prevention and treatment are complementary, interdependent, and united in their contribution to developing prosocial behavior. The cost savings are not necessarily because prevention obviates the need for treatment, but rather because a broad range of intervention opportunities are required to achieve significant impact on the costly, burdensome social problem that aggressive and antisocial behavior represents.

Beyond Prevention and Treatment

Prevention and treatment efforts are obviously important, but they must work against significant obstacles embedded in everyday life. There are multiple opportunities to reduce influences that can contribute to conduct problems and aggression more generally. For example, the use of corporal punishment in child-rearing and school discipline; violence in the media, especially television and films; and social practices that permit, facilitate, or tacitly condone violence and aggression (e.g., availability of weapons) are some of the practices that are relevant to the issue of aggression and antisocial behavior in society. As a matter of social policy, we take as given a backdrop of factors and practices that contribute in significant ways to aggression and antisocial behavior in society. The factors need to be scrutinized in relation to policy regarding child management and care.

For example, the use of corporal punishment (i.e., physical aggression against children) is already implicated as a contributor to child aggression. The extensive use of corporal punishment is one of the givens in our society—a right that accompanies parenting and often teaching —that might be challenged if there were broad interest in delimiting aggression and antisocial behavior. In this regard, it is instructive to note that corporal punishment in child discipline at home and at school has been banned in a number of countries (e.g., Austria, Denmark, Finland, Norway, and Sweden; Greven, 1992). Social efforts to reduce aggression and violence on a large scale are no less important than interventions developed, implemented, and evaluated in the context of small-scale prevention and treatment trials.

Influences that might affect violence (e.g., gun control, limits of permissible violence on television, reduced violence and violent superheros in films) often are discussed in the media as well as in policy deliberations. Efforts to limit aggression and violence in everyday life are particularly difficult because they clash with specific constitutional rights, or with the perception and interpretation of such rights. A more difficult obstacle in setting policy may come from oversimplistic interpretations of individual influences. For example, one might argue for strong gun control as one means to influence aggression and violence. The standard counterargument is that the presence of guns and their misuse account for relatively little violence or are not the cause or main influence on aggression in society. From a policy standpoint, such logic warrants more critical analysis.

No one influence accounts for, or causes, aggression and antisocial behavior. It might be useful to conceptualize the full range of influences in terms of a risk-factor model in which there are multiple influences that contribute to some outcome. In this case, the outcome is the overall level and type of aggression in society. We do not look for single, simple causes, but rather seek to identify a range of influences. Even influences that are arguably small in their impact on the outcome (e.g., small beta weight in a regression equation) can be exceedingly important in terms of social impact. In a risk-factor model, multiple influences add and combine to increase the likelihood of the outcome (e.g., aggression). Small influences can combine and add appreciably, even though their individual contribution would be nugatory. Also, individual influences can interact (or synergistically combine) with other influences and very much affect the outcome. We want to reduce risk factors not because individually they are *the* cause or because they will *eliminate* the problem, but because they will have palpable impact.

The preceding argument suggests that small influences are, nevertheless, important. Yet one could push the argument well beyond this. Many influences cast aside as small might be argued as actually quite strong and increase the urgency for intervention and attention. For example, efforts to quell detailed, pervasive, and frequent violence in the media are countered with another set of arguments noting the benefits of television (e.g., education) and the responsibilities of others (e.g., parents) in policing what children watch. Yet one set of arguments does not gainsay the others. The impact of the media on antisocial and at-risk behaviors has been documented and that impact is not trivial (see

Strasburger, 1995). One might argue that labeling and classifying different types of movies or television shows, for example, based on their level of violence is not likely to be the intervention to affect their impact or the audience they reach. The task of reducing violence in childhood and adolescence does not mean that only that level is the focus. The task of reducing violence at all other levels (e.g., spouse abuse, media to which adults are exposed) is likely to have broader impact. However, this type of discussion enters into areas that go well beyond what is permitted or, for many, even desired, in a free society.

As a matter of policy, it would be worthwhile to make a legislative and social commitment to the reduction of aggression and violence in society. Prevention and treatment programs of the type reviewed in earlier chapters are important but in this larger context quite limited. Much more extensive broad-based programs are also needed. In a different social setting and context, the program in Norway (Olweus, 1991), designed to reduce bullying, represents an effort along such lines. The specifics of that program or the applicability of the details to different countries are not the issues. Rather the intervention represents a multiple-component effort at the level of public policy to ameliorate the problem. A commitment at the policy level and at the level that can mobilize social forces that influence, express, or model aggression could also have significant impact on the problem. Social influences involving the matrix of societal displays, encouragement, and implicit endorsement of aggression including the media at all levels ought to be mobilized more systematically for a broad effort to ameliorate aggression and antisocial behavior. Again, this is not the solution nor a reflection on the cause of aggression in society, but rather a way to have impact in one more incremental way.

This book has focused on the dysfunction among children and adolescents and their families. The range of factors that influence the emergence of conduct disorder is broad. The breadth raised not only suggests the complexity of the problem but also points to possible areas of intervention to produce change.

NOTES

1. Child abuse is an interesting example. Researchers often select abused individuals from child youth services in which cases are identified. One of the problems is that child abuse is defined legally by such services, so that families are identified whose abuse meets the legal definition (e.g., hitting children with objects, incurring

physical marks or injuries from corporal punishment). (These definitions are devised by individual states within the United States, and hence a great deal of variation may occur among them.) The point is that child abuse is not necessarily a problem only when the threshold of the legal definition is met. The use of corporal punishment can be viewed along continua, such as frequency and severity of the punishment and threshold for its use (i.e., what the child has to do to provoke abusive punishment). The legal definition of abuse is quite extreme, and understandably so perhaps. The legal issue is the extent to which the state wishes (and is able from cost standpoints) to intervene. From a developmental standpoint, consequences to the child (including risk for later violence and conduct disorder) probably occur well before the level of severity that meets the legal definition. To understand how abuse operates requires evaluation of cases along the entire spectrum of child-rearing practices.

    2. The Conduct Problem Prevention Group includes Karen L. Bierman, John D. Coie, Kenneth A. Dodge, Mark T. Greenberg, John E. Lochman, and Robert J. McMahon.

REFERENCES

Achenbach, T. M. (1991). *Manual for the Child Behavior Checklist/4-18 and 1991 Profile.* Burlington: University of Vermont, Department of Psychiatry.

Achenbach, T. M. (1993a). *Empirically based taxonomy: How to use syndromes and profile types derived from the CBCL/4-18, TRF, and YSR.* Burlington, VT: University Associates in Psychiatry.

Achenbach, T. M. (1993b). Taxonomy and comorbidity of conduct problems: Evidence from empirically based approaches. *Development and Psychopathology, 5,* 51-64.

Achenbach, T. M., McConaughy, S. H., & Howell, C. T. (1987). Child/adolescent behavioral and emotional problems: Implications of cross-informant correlations for situational specificity. *Psychological Bulletin, 101,* 213-232.

Adams, S. (1970). The PICO project. In N. Johnston, L. Savitz, & M. E. Wolfgang (Eds.), *The sociology of punishment and correction* (pp. 548-561). New York: John Wiley.

Alexander, J. F., Barton, C., Schiavo, R. S., & Parsons, B. V. (1976). Systems-behavioral intervention with families of delinquents: Therapist characteristics, family behavior, and outcome. *Journal of Consulting and Clinical Psychology, 44,* 656-664.

Alexander, J. F., Holtzworth-Munroe, A., & Jameson, P. B. (1994). The process and outcome of marital and family therapy research: Review and evaluation. In A. E. Bergin & S. L. Garfield (Eds.), *Handbook of psychotherapy and behavior change* (4th ed., pp. 595-630). New York: John Wiley.

Alexander, J. F., & Parsons, B. V. (1982). *Functional family therapy.* Monterey, CA: Brooks/Cole.

Allen, J. P., Philliber, S., & Hoggson, N. (1990). School-based prevention of teen-age pregnancy and school dropout: Process evaluation of the national replication of the Teen Outreach Program. *American Journal of Community Psychology, 18,* 505-524.

American Psychiatric Association. (1994). *Diagnostic and statistical manual of mental disorders* (4th ed.). Washington, DC: Author.

American Psychological Association, Commission on Violence and Youth. (1993). *Violence and youth: Psychology's response* (Vol. 1). Washington, DC: Author.

Bachman, J. G., Johnston, L. D., & O'Malley, P. M. (1978). Delinquent behavior linked to educational attainment and post-high school experiences. In L. Otten (Ed.), *Colloquium on the correlates of crime and the determinants of criminal behavior* (pp. 1-43). Arlington, VA: The MITRE Corp.

Baer, R. A., & Nietzel, M. T. (1991). Cognitive and behavioral treatment of impulsivity in children: A meta-analytic review of the outcome literature. *Journal of Clinical Child Psychology, 20,* 400-412.

Bangert-Drowns, R. L. (1988). The effects of school-based substance abuse education: A meta-analysis. *Journal of Drug Education, 18,* 243-264.

Bank, L., Marlowe, J. H., Reid, J. B., Patterson, G. R., & Weinrott, M. R. (1991). A comparative evaluation of parent-training interventions for families of chronic delinquents. *Journal of Abnormal Child Psychology, 19,* 15-33.

Barkley, R. A. (1988). Child behavior rating scales. In M. Rutter, A. H. Tuma, & I. S. Lann (Eds.), *Assessment and diagnosis in child psychopathology* (pp. 113-155). New York: Guilford.

Behar, D., & Stewart, M. A. (1982). Aggressive conduct disorder of children. *Acta Psychiatrica Scandinavica, 65,* 210-220.

Bell, R. Q., & Harper, L. (1977). *Child effects on adults.* New York: John Wiley.

Bien, N. Z., & Bry, B. H. (1980). An experimentally designed comparison of four intensities of school-based prevention programs for adolescents with adjustment problems. *Journal of Community Psychology, 8,* 110-116.

Blashfield, R. K. (1984). *The classification of psychopathology: Neo-Kraepelinian and quantitative approaches.* New York: Plenum.

Booth, C. L., Spieker, S. J., Barnard, K. E., & Morriset, C. E. (1992). Infants at risk: The role of preventive inervention in deflecting a maladaptive developmental trajectory. In J. McCord & R. E. Tremblay (Eds.), *Preventing antisocial behavior* (pp. 21-42). New York: Guilford.

Botvin, G. J., Baker, E., Filazzola, A. D., & Botvin, F. M. (1990). A cognitive-behavioral approach to substance abuse prevention: One-year follow-up. *Addictive Behaviors, 15,* 47-63.

Boyle, M. H., & Offord, D. R. (1990). Primary prevention of conduct disorder: Issues and prospects. *Journal of the American Academy of Child and Adolescent Psychiatry, 29,* 227-233.

Brandt, D. E., & Zlotnick, S. J. (1988). *The psychology and treatment of the youthful offender.* Springfield, IL: Charles C Thomas.

Brennan, P., Mednick, S., & Kandel, E. (1991). Congenital determinants of violent and property offending. In D. J. Pepler & K. H. Rubin (Eds.), *The development and treatment of childhood aggression* (pp. 79-92). Hillsdale, NJ: Lawrence Erlbaum.

Buckner, J. C., & Chesney-Lind, M. (1983). Dramatic cures for juvenile crime: An evaluation of a prisoner-run delinquency prevention program. *Criminal Justice and Behavior, 10,* 227-247.

Cadoret, R. J. (1978). Psychopathology in adopted-away offspring of biological parents with antisocial behavior. *Archives of General Psychiatry, 35,* 176-184.

Cadoret, R. J., & Cain, C. (1980). Sex differences in predictors of antisocial behavior in adoptees. *Archives of General Psychiatry, 37,* 1171-1175.

Cadoret, R. J., & Cain, C. (1981). Environmental and genetic factors in predicting adolescent antisocial behavior. *The Psychiatric Journal of the University of Ottawa, 6,* 220-225.

Cadoret, R. J., Cain, C., & Crowe, R. R. (1983). Evidence for gene-environment interaction in the development of adolescent antisocial behavior. *Behavior Genetics, 13,* 301-310.

Carlson, C. L., Lahey, B. B., & Neeper, R. (1984). Peer assessment of the social behavior of accepted, rejected, and neglected children. *Journal of Abnormal Child Psychology, 12,* 189-198.

Casey, R. J., & Berman, J. S. (1985). The outcome of psychotherapy with children. *Psychological Bulletin, 98,* 388-400.

Catalano, R. F., Hawkins, J. D., Krenz, C., Gillmore, M., Morrison, D., Wells, E., & Abbott, R. (1993). Using research to guide culturally appropriate drug abuse prevention. *Journal of Consulting and Clinical Psychology, 61,* 804-811.

Chamberlain, P., & Reid, P. (1987). Parent observation and report of child symptoms. *Behavioral Assessment, 9,* 97-109.

Cicchetti, D., & Garmezy, N. (Eds.). (1993). Special Issue: Milestones in the development of resilience. *Development and Psychopathology, 5,* 497-783.

Cloninger, C. R., Reich, T., & Guze, S. B. (1978). Genetic-environmental interactions and antisocial behaviour. In R. D. Hare & D. Schalling (Eds.), *Psychopathic behaviour: Approaches to research* (pp. 225-237). Chichester, UK: John Wiley.

Coie, J., Lochman, J. E., Terry, R., & Hyman, C. (1992). Predicting early adolescent disorder from childhood aggression and peer rejection. *Journal of Consulting and Clinical Psychology, 60,* 783-792.

Conduct Problems Prevention Research Group. (1992). A developmental and clinical model for prevention of conduct disorder. *Development and Psychopathology, 4,* 509-527.

Constantino, J. N., Grosz, D., Saenger, P., Chandler, D. W., Nandi, R., & Earls, F. J. (1993). Testosterone and aggression in children. *Journal of the American Academy of Child and Adolescent Psychiatry, 32,* 1217-1222.

Crick, N. R., & Dodge, K. A. (1994). A review and reformulation of social information processing mechanisms in children's social adjustment. *Psychological Bulletin, 115,* 74-101.

Crowe, R. R. (1974). An adoption study of antisocial personality. *Archives of General Psychiatry, 31,* 785-791.

Curtiss, G., Rosenthal, R. H., Marohn, R. C., Ostrov, E., Offer, D., & Trujillo, J. (1983). Measuring delinquent behavior in inpatient treatment settings: Revision and validation of the Adolescent Antisocial Behavior Checklist. *Journal of the American Academy of Child Psychiatry, 22,* 459-466.

Dadds, M. R., & McHugh, T. A. (1992). Social support and treatment outcome in behavioral family therapy for child conduct problems. *Journal of Consulting and Clinical Psychology, 60,* 252-259.

Dadds, M. R., Schwartz, S., & Sanders, M. R. (1987). Marital discord and treatment outcome in behavioral treatment of child conduct disorders. *Journal of Consulting and Clinical Psychology, 55,* 396-403.

Davidson, W. S., II, & Redner, R. (1988). The prevention of juvenile delinquency: Diversion from the juvenile justice system. In R. H. Price, E. L. Cowen, R. P. Lorion, & J. Ramos-McKay (Eds.), *14 ounces of prevention: A casebook for practitioners* (pp. 123-137). Washington, DC: American Psychological Association.

Davidson, W. S., II, Redner, R., Blakely, C. H., Mitchell, C. M., & Emshoff, J. G. (1987). Diversion of juvenile offenders: An experimental comparison. *Journal of Consulting and Clinical Psychology, 55,* 68-75.

Day, D. M., Bream, L. A., & Pal, A. (1992). Proactive and reactive aggression: An analysis of subtypes based on teacher perceptions. *Journal of Clinical Child Psychology, 21,* 210-217.

Deluty, R. H. (1979). Children's Action Tendency Scale: A self-report measure of aggressiveness, assertiveness, and submissiveness in children. *Journal of Consulting and Clinical Psychology, 47,* 1061-1071.

DiLalla, L. F., & Gottesman, I. I. (1989). Heterogeneity of causes for delinquency and criminality: Lifespan perspectives. *Development and Psychopathology, 1,* 339-349.

Dishion, T. J., & Patterson, G. R. (1992). Age effects in parent training outcomes. *Behavior Therapy, 23,* 719-729.

Dishion, T. J., Patterson, G. R., & Kavanagh, K. A. (1992). An experimental test of the coercion model: Linking theory, measurement, and intervention. In J. McCord & R. E. Tremblay (Eds.), *Preventing antisocial behavior* (pp. 253-282). New York: Guilford.

Dodge, K. A. (1985). Attributional bias in aggressive children. In P. C. Kendall (Ed.), *Advances in cognitive-behavioral research and therapy* (Vol. 4, pp. 75-110). Orlando, FL: Academic Press.

Dodge, K. A. (1991). The structure and function of reactive and proactive aggression. In D. J. Pepler & K. H. Rubin (Eds.), *The development and treatment of childhood aggression* (pp. 201-218). Hillsdale, NJ: Lawrence Erlbaum.

Dumas, J. E. (1989). Treating antisocial behavior in children: Child and family approaches. *Clinical Psychology Review, 9,* 197-222.

Dumas, J. E., & Wahler, R. G. (1983). Predictors of treatment outcome in parent training: Mother insularity and socioeconomic disadvantage. *Behavioral Assessment, 5,* 301-313.

Durlak, J. A., Fuhrman, T., & Lampman, C. (1991). Effectiveness of cognitive-behavioral therapy for maladapting children: A meta analysis. *Psychological Bulletin, 110,* 204-214.

Elliott, D. S., Dunford, F. W., & Huizinga, D. (1987). The identification and prediction of career offenders utilizing self-reported and official data. In J. D. Burchard & S. N. Burchard (Eds.), *Preventing delinquent behavior* (pp. 90-121). Newbury Park, CA: Sage.

Elliott, D. S., Huizinga, D., & Ageton, S. S. (1985). *Explaining delinquency and drug use.* Beverly Hills, CA: Sage.

Elliott, D. S., Huizinga, D., & Menard, S. (1988). *Multiple problem youth: Delinquency, substance abuse, and mental health problems.* New York: Springer-Verlag.

Empey, L. T. (1982). *American delinquency: Its meaning and construction.* Homewood, IL: Dorsey.

Eron, L. D., Huesmann, L. R., & Zelli, A. (1991). The role of parental variables in the learning of aggression. In D. J. Pepler & K. H. Rubin (Eds.), *The development and treatment of childhood aggression* (pp. 169-188). Hillsdale, NJ: Lawrence Erlbaum.

Eyberg, S. M., & Robinson, E. A. (1983). Conduct problem behavior: Standardization of a behavioral rating scale with adolescents. *Journal of Clinical Child Psychology, 12,* 347-354.

Farrington, D. P. (1978). The family backgrounds of aggressive youths. In L. A. Hersov, M. Berger, & D. Shaffer (Eds.), *Aggression and anti-social behaviour in childhood and adolescence* (pp. 73-93). Oxford, UK: Pergamon.

Farrington, D. P. (1984). Measuring the natural history of delinquency and crime. In R. A. Glow (Ed.), *Advances in the behavioral measurement of children* (Vol. 1, pp. 217-263). Greenwich, CT: JAI Press.

Farrington, D. P. (1985). Predicting self-reported and official delinquency. In D. P. Farrington & R. Tarling (Eds.), *Prediction in criminology* (pp. 150-173). Albany, NY: SUNY.

Farrington, D. P. (1991). Childhood aggression and adult violence: Early precursors and later life outcomes. In D. J. Pepler & K. H. Rubin (Eds.), *The development and treatment of childhood aggression* (pp. 5-29). Hillsdale, NJ: Lawrence Erlbaum.

Farrington, D. P., & Hawkins, J. D. (1991). Predicting participation, early onset and later persistence in officially recorded offending. *Criminal Behavior and Mental Health, 1,* 1-33.

Feldman, R. A. (1992). The St. Louis experiment: Effective treatment of antisocial youths in prosocial peer groups. In J. McCord & R. E. Tremblay (Eds.), *Preventing antisocial behavior* (pp. 233-252). New York: Guilford.

Feldman, R. A., Caplinger, T. E., & Wodarski, J. S. (1983). *The St. Louis conundrum: The effective treatment of antisocial youths.* Englewood Cliffs, NJ: Prentice Hall.

Felner, R. D., & Adan, A. M. (1988). The school transitional environment project: An ecological intervention and evaluation. In R. H. Price, E. L. Cowen, R. P. Lorion, & J. Ramos-McKay (Eds.), *14 ounces of prevention: A casebook for practitioners* (pp. 111-122). Washington, DC: American Psychological Association.

Fergusson, D. M., Horwood, L. J., & Lloyd, M. (1991). Confirmatory factor models of attention deficit and conduct disorder. *Journal of Child Psychology and Psychiatry, 32,* 257-274.

Finch, A. J., Jr., Nelson, W. M., III., & Ott, E. S. (1993). *Cognitive-behavioral procedures with children and adolescents: A practical guide.* Needham Heights, MA: Allyn & Bacon.

Finckenauer, J. O. (1982). *Scared straight! and the panacea phenomenon.* Englewood Cliffs, NJ: Prentice Hall.

Fo, W. S. O., & O'Donnell, C. R. (1975). The buddy system: Effect of community intervention on delinquent offenses. *Behavior Therapy, 6,* 522-524.

Forehand, R., & Long, N. (1988). Outpatient treatment of the acting out child: Procedures, long-term follow-up data, and clinical problems. *Advances in Behaviour Research and Therapy, 10,* 129-177.

Forehand, R., & McMahon, R. J. (1981). *Helping the noncompliant child: A clinician's guide to parent training.* New York: Guilford.

Frick, P. J., & Jackson, Y. K. (1993). Family functioning and childhood antisocial behavior: Yet another reinterpretation. *Journal of Clinical Child Psychology, 22,* 410-419.

Funderburk, B. W., & Eyberg, S. M. (1989). Psychometric characteristics of the Sutter-Eyberg Student Behavior Inventory: A school behavior rating scale for use with preschool children. *Behavioral Assessment, 11,* 297-313.

Galloway, D. (1985). *Schools and persistent absentees.* Oxford, UK: Pergamon.

Garmezy, N. (1985). Stress-resistant children: The search for protective factors. In J. E. Stevenson (Ed.), *Recent research in developmental psychopathology* (pp. 213-233). Oxford, UK: Pergamon.

Glidewell, J. C. (1983). Prevention: The threat and the promise. In R. D. Felner, L. A. Jason, J. N. Moritsugu, & S. S. Farber (Eds.), *Preventive psychology: Theory, research and practice* (pp. 310-312). New York: Pergamon.

Glueck, S., & Glueck, E. (1968). *Delinquents and nondelinquents in perspective.* Cambridge, MA: Harvard University Press.

Goldston, S. E., Yager, J., Heinicke, C. M., & Pynoos, R. S. (Eds.). (1990). *Preventing mental health disturbances in childhood.* Washington, DC: American Psychiatric Press.

Gottesman, I. I., Carey, G., & Hanson, D. R. (1983). Pearls and perils in epigenetic psychopathology. In S. B. Guze, E. J. Earls, & J. E. Barrett (Eds.), *Childhood psychopathology and development* (pp. 287-300). New York: Raven.

Graham, J. R. (1990). *MMPI-2: Assessing personality and psychopathology.* New York: Oxford University Press.

Greven, P. (1992). Exploring the effects of corporal punishment. *Child, Youth, and Family Services Quarterly, 15*(4), 4-5.

Griest, D. L., Forehand, R., Rogers, T., Breiner, J., Furey, W., & Williams, C. A. (1982). Effects of parent enhancement therapy on the treatment outcome and generalization of a parent training program. *Behaviour Research and Therapy, 20,* 429-436.

Hawkins, J. D., Catalano, R. F., & Miller, J. Y. (1992). Risk and protective factors for alcohol and other drug problems in adolescence and early adulthood: Implications for substance abuse prevention. *Psychological Bulletin, 112,* 64-105.

Hawkins, J. D., Catalano, R. F., Morrison, D. M., O'Donnell, J. O., Abbott, R. D., & Day, L. E. (1992). The Seattle social development project: Effects of the first four years on protective factors and problem behaviors. In J. McCord & R. E. Tremblay (Eds.), *Preventing antisocial behavior* (pp. 139-161). New York: Guilford.

Hawkins, J. D., Doueck, H. J., & Lishner, D. M. (1988). Changing teaching practices in mainstream classrooms to improve bonding and behavior of low achievers. *American Educational Research Journal, 25,* 31-50.

Hawkins, J. D., & Lam, T. (1987). Teacher practices, social development, and delinquency. In J. D. Burchard & S. N. Burchard (Eds.), *Prevention of delinquent behavior* (pp. 241-274). Newbury Park, CA: Sage.

Hawkins, J. D., Von Cleve, E., & Catalano, R. F. (1991). Reducing early childhood aggression: Results of a primary prevention program. *Journal of the American Academy of Child and Adolescent Psychiatry, 30,* 208-217.

Henggeler, S. W. (1989). *Delinquency in adolescence.* Newbury Park, CA: Sage.

Henggeler, S. W. (1994). *Treatment manual for family preservation using multisystemic therapy.* Charleston: Medical University of South Carolina, South Carolina Health and Human Services Finance Commission.

Henggeler, S. W., & Borduin, C. M. (1990). *Family therapy and beyond: A multisystemic approach to teaching the behavior problems of children and adolescents.* Pacific Grove, CA: Brooks/Cole.

Henggeler, S. W., Melton, G. B., & Smith, L. A. (1992). Family preservation using multisystemic therapy: An effective alternative to incarcerating serious juvenile offenders. *Journal of Consulting and Clinical Psychology, 60,* 953-961.

Henggeler, S. W., Rodick, J. D., Borduin, C. M., Hanson, C. L., Watson, S. M., & Urey, J. R. (1986). Multisystemic treatment of juvenile offenders: Effects on adolescent behavior and family interaction. *Developmental Psychology, 22,* 132-141.

Hetherington, E. M., Cox, M., & Cox, R. (1982). Effects of divorce on parents and children. In M. Lamb (Ed.), *Nontraditional families* (pp. 223-288). Hillsdale, NJ: Lawrence Erlbaum.

Hinshaw, S. P. (1991). Stimulant medication and the treatment of aggression in children with attentional deficits. *Journal of Clinical Child Psychology, 20,* 301-312.

Hinshaw, S. P., Heller, T., & McHale, J. P. (1992). Covert antisocial behavior in boys with Attention-Deficit Hyperactivity Disorder: External validation and effects of methylphenidate. *Journal of Consulting and Clinical Psychology, 60,* 274-281.

Hinshaw, S. P., Lahey, B. B., & Hart, E. L. (1993). Issues of taxonomy and comorbidity in the development of conduct disorder. *Development and Psychopathology, 5,* 31-49.

Hodges, K., & Zeman, J. (1993). Interviewing. In T. H. Ollendick & M. Hersen (Eds.), *Handbook of child and adolescent assessment* (pp. 65-81). Needham Heights, MA: Allyn & Bacon.

Huesmann, L. R., Eron, L. D., Lefkowitz, M. M., & Walder, L. O. (1984). Stability of aggression over time and generations. *Developmental Psychology, 20,* 1120-1134.

Institute of Medicine. (1989). *Research on children and adolescents with mental, behavioral, and developmental disorders.* Washington, DC: National Academy Press.

Jaffe, P. G., Hurley, D. J., & Wolfe, D. (1990). Children's observations of violence: I. Critical issues in child development and intervention planning. *Canadian Journal of Psychiatry, 35,* 466-170.

Jessor, R., Donovan, J. E., & Costa, F. M. (1991). *Beyond adolescence: Problem behavior and young adult development.* Cambridge, UK: Cambridge University Press.

Jessor, R., & Jessor, S. L. (1977). *Problem behavior and psychological development: A longitudinal study of youth.* New York: Academic Press.

Johnson, D. L. (1988). Primary prevention of behavior problems in young children: The Houston parent-child development center. In R. H. Price, E. L. Cowen, R. P. Lorion, & J. Ramos-McKay (Eds.), *14 ounces of prevention: A casebook for practitioners* (pp. 44-52). Washington, DC: American Psychological Association.

Kagan, J. (1969). The three faces of continuity in human development. In D. A. Goslin (Ed.), *Handbook of socialization theory and research* (pp. 983-1002). Chicago: Rand McNally.

Kazdin, A. E. (1985). *Treatment of antisocial behavior in children and adolescents.* Homewood, IL: Dorsey Press.

Kazdin, A. E. (1988). *Child psychotherapy: Developing and identifying effective treatments.* Needham Heights, MA: Allyn & Bacon.

Kazdin, A. E. (1992a). Overt and covert antisocial behavior: Child and family characteristics among psychiatric inpatient children. *Journal of Child and Family Studies, 1,* 3-20.

Kazdin, A. E. (1992b). *Research design in clinical psychology* (2nd ed.). Needham Heights, MA: Allyn & Bacon.

Kazdin, A. E. (1993). Treatment of conduct disorder: Progress and directions in psychotherapy research. *Development and Psychopathology, 5,* 277-310.

Kazdin, A. E. (1994). Informant variability in the assessment of childhood depression. In W. M. Reynolds & H. Johnston (Eds.), *Handbook of depression in children and adolescents.* New York: Plenum.

Kazdin, A. E. (in press). Child, parent, and family dysfunction as predictors of outcome in cognitive-behavioral treatment of antisocial children. *Behaviour Research and Therapy.*

Kazdin, A. E., Bass, D., Ayers, W. A., & Rodgers, A. (1990). Empirical and clinical focus of child and adolescent psychotherapy research. *Journal of Consulting and Clinical Psychology, 58,* 729-740.

Kazdin, A. E., Bass, D., Siegel, T., & Thomas, C. (1989). Cognitive-behavioral treatment and relationship therapy in the treatment of children referred for antisocial behavior. *Journal of Consulting and Clinical Psychology, 57,* 522-535.

Kazdin, A. E., & Esveldt-Dawson, K. (1986). The interview for antisocial behavior: Psychometric characteristics and concurrent validity with child psychiatric inpatients. *Journal of Psychopathology and Behavioral Assessment, 8,* 289-303.

Kazdin, A. E., & Kagan, J. (1994). Models of dysfunction in developmental psychopathology. *Clinical Psychology: Science and Practice, 1,* 35-52.

Kazdin, A. E., Rodgers, A., Colbus, D., & Siegel, T. (1987). Children's Hostility Inventory: Measurement of aggression and hostility in psychiatric inpatient children. *Journal of Clinical Child Psychology, 16,* 320-328.

Kazdin, A. E., Siegel, T. C., & Bass, D. (1990). Drawing upon clinical practice to inform research on child and adolescent psychotherapy: A survey of practitioners. *Professional Psychology: Research and Practice, 21,* 189-198.

Kazdin, A. E., Siegel, T., & Bass, D. (1992). Cognitive problem-solving skills training and parent management training in the treatment of antisocial behavior in children. *Journal of Consulting and Clinical Psychology, 60,* 733-747.

Kendall, P. C. (Ed.). (1991). *Child and adolescent therapy: Cognitive-behavioral procedures.* New York: Guilford.

Kolko, D. J., & Kazdin, A. E. (1986). Conceptualization of firesetting in children and adolescents. *Journal of Abnormal Child Psychology, 14,* 49-61.

Kolko, D. J., & Kazdin, A. E. (1992). The emergence and recurrence of child firesetting: A one-year prospective study. *Journal of Abnormal Child Psychology, 20,* 17-37.

Kolvin, I., Miller, F. J. W., Fleeting, J., & Kolvin, P. A. (1988). Social and parenting factors affecting criminal offense rates: Findings from the Newcastle thousand family study (1947-1980). *British Journal of Psychiatry, 152,* 80-90.

Kruesi, M. J. P., Hibbs, E. D., Zahn, T. P., Keysor, C. S., Hamburger, S. D., Bartko, J. J., & Rapoport, J. L. (1992). A two-year prospective folllow-up study of children and adolescents with disruptive behavior disorders: Prediction by cerebrospinal fluid 5-hydroxyindoleacetic acid, homovanillic acid, and autonomic measures. *Archives of General Psychiatry, 49,* 429-435.

Kruesi, M. J. P., Rapoport, J. L., Hamburger, S. D., Hibbs, E. D., Potter, W. Z., Lenare, M., & Brown, G. L. (1990). Cerebrospinal fluid monoamine metabolites, aggression, and impulsivity in disruptive behavior disorders of children and adolescents. *Archives of General Psychiatry, 47,* 419-426.

Kulik, J. A., Stein, K. B., & Sarbin, T. R. (1968). Dimensions and patterns of adolescent antisocial behavior. *Journal of Consulting and Clinical Psychology, 32,* 375-382.

Kupfer, D. J., Frank, E., Perel, J. M., Cornes, C., Mallinger, A. G., Thase, M. E., McEachran, A. B., & Grochocinski, V. J. (1992). Five-year outcome for maintenance therapies in recurrent depression. *Archives of General Psychiatry, 49,* 769-773.

Lahey, B. B., Hart, E. L., Pliszka, S., Applegate, B., & McBurnett, K. (1993). Neurophysiological correlates of conduct disorder: A rationale and a review of research. *Journal of Clinical Child Psychology, 22,* 141-153.

Lahey, B. B., Loeber, R., Quay, H. C., Frick, P. J., & Grimm, J. (1992). Oppositional defiant and conduct disorders: Issues to be resolved for *DSM-IV*. *Journal of the American Academy of Child and Adolescent Psychiatry, 31*, 539-546.

Lally, R., Mangione, P. L., & Honig, A. S. (1988). The Syracuse University Family Development Research Program: Long-range impact on an early intervention with low-income children and their families. In D. Powell (Ed.), *Parent education as early childhood intervention: Emerging directions in theory, research, and practice* (pp. 79-104). Norwood, NJ: Ablex.

Ledingham, J. E., & Schwartzman, A. E. (1984). A 3-year follow-up of aggressive and withdrawn behavior in childhood: Preliminary findings. *Journal of Abnormal Child Psychology, 12*, 157-168.

Lefkowitz, M. M., Eron, L. D., Walder, L. O., & Huesmann, L. R. (1977). *Growing up to be violent: A longitudinal study of the development of aggression.* New York: Pergamon.

Levenstein, P. (1992). The mother-child home program: Research methodology and the real world. In J. McCord & R. E. Tremblay (Eds.), *Preventing antisocial behavior* (pp. 43-66). New York: Guilford.

Lewis, D. O. (1992). From abuse to violence: Psychophysiological consequences of maltreatment. *Journal of the American Academy of Child and Adolescent Psychiatry, 31*, 383-391.

Lochman, J. E., & Dodge, K. A. (1994). Social-cognitive processes of severely violent, moderately aggressive, and nonaggressive boys. *Journal of Consulting and Clinical Psychology, 62*, 366-374.

Loeber, R. (1990). Development and risk factors of juvenile antisocial behavior and delinquency. *Clinical Psychology Review, 10*, 1-41.

Loeber, R., & Dishion, T. J. (1983). Early predictors of male delinquency: A review. *Psychological Bulletin, 94*, 68-99.

Loeber, R., Keenan, K., Lahey, B. B., Green, S. M., & Thomas, C. (1993). Evidence for developmentally based diagnoses of oppositional defiant disorder and conduct disorder. *Journal of Abnormal Child Psychology, 21*, 377-410.

Loeber, R., Lahey, B. B., & Thomas, C. (1991). Diagnostic conundrum of oppositional defiant disorder and conduct disorder. *Journal of Abnormal Psychology, 100*, 379-390.

Loeber, R., & Schmaling, K. B. (1985). Empirical evidence for overt and covert patterns of antisocial conduct problems: A meta-analysis. *Journal of Abnormal Child Psychology, 13*, 337-352.

Loeber, R., Wung, P., Keenan, K., Giroux, B., Stouthamer-Loeber, M., Van Kammen, W. B., & Maughan, B. (1993). Developmental pathways in disruptive child behavior. *Development and Psychopathology, 5*, 103-133.

Long, P., Forehand, R., Wierson, M., & Morgan, A. (1994). Does parent training with young noncompliant children have long-term effects? *Behaviour Research and Therapy, 32*, 101-107.

Lundman, R. J. (1984). *Prevention and control of juvenile delinquency.* New York: Oxford University Press.

Lytton, H. (1990). Child and parent effects in boys' conduct disorder: A reinterpretation. *Developmental Psychology, 26*, 683-697.

Maccoby, E. E. (1986). Social groupings in childhood: Their relationship to prosocial and antisocial behavior in boys and girls. In D. Olweus, J. Block, & M. Radke-

Yarrow (Eds.), *Development of antisocial and prosocial behavior* (pp. 263-284). Orlando, FL: Academic Press.

MacFarlane, J. W., Allen, L., & Honzik, M. P. (1954). *A developmental study of the behavior problems of normal children between 21 months and 14 years.* Berkeley: University of California Press.

Maddahian, E., Newcomb, M. D., & Bentler, P. M. (1988). Risk factors for substance use: Ethnic differences among adolescents. *Journal of Substance Abuse, 1,* 11-23.

Mann, B. J., Borduin, C. M., Henggeler, S. W., & Blaske, D. M. (1990). An investigation of systemic conceptualizations of parent-child coalitions and symptom change. *Journal of Consulting and Clinical Psychology, 58,* 336-344.

Maser, J. D., Kaelber, C., & Weise, R. E. (1991). International use and attitudes toward *DSM-III* and *DSM-III-R*: Growing consensus in psychiatric classification. *Journal of Abnormal Psychology, 100,* 271-279.

Mattsson, A., Schalling, D., Olweus, D., Low, H., & Svensson, J. (1980). Plasma testosterone, aggressive behavior, and personality dimensions in young male delinquents. *Journal of the American Academy of Child Psychiatry, 19,* 476-490.

McConaughy, S. H. (1992). Objective assessment of children's behavioral and emotional problems. In C. E. Walker & M. C. Roberts (Eds.), *Handbook of clinical child psychology* (2nd ed., pp. 163-180). New York: John Wiley.

McCord, J. (1978). A thirty-year follow-up of treatment effects. *American Psychologist, 33,* 284-289.

McCord, W., McCord, J., & Zola, I. K. (1959). *Origins of crime.* New York: Columbia University Press.

McCord, J., & Tremblay, R. E. (Eds.). (1992). *Preventing antisocial behavior.* New York: Guilford.

McGee, L., & Newcomb, M. D. (1992). General deviance syndrome: Expanded hierarchical evaluations at four ages from early adolescence to adulthood. *Journal of Consulting and Clinical Psychology, 60,* 766-776.

McGee, R., Feehan, M., Williams, S., & Anderson, J. (1992). *DSM-III* disorders from age 11-15 years. *Journal of the American Academy of Child and Adolescent Psychiatry, 31,* 50-59.

McMahon, R. J., & Forehand, R. (1988). Conduct disorders. In E. J. Mash & L. G. Terdal (Eds.), *Behavioral assessment of childhood disorders* (2nd ed., pp. 105-153). New York: Guilford.

Meisels, S. J., & Shonkoff, J. P. (Eds.). (1990). *Handbook of early childhood intervention.* Cambridge: Cambridge University Press.

Miller, G. E., & Prinz, R. J. (1990). Enhancement of social learning family interventions for child conduct disorder. *Psychological Bulletin, 108,* 291-307.

Moffitt, T. E. (1993a). Adolescence-limited and life-course persistent antisocial behavior: A developmental taxonomy. *Psychological Review, 100,* 674-701.

Moffitt, T. E. (1993b). The neuropsychology of conduct disorder. *Development and Psychopathology, 5,* 135-151.

Moore, D. R., Chamberlain, P., & Mukai, L. H. (1979). Children at risk for delinquency: A follow-up comparison of aggressive children and children who steal. *Journal of Abnormal Child Psychology, 7,* 345-355.

Morris, S. M., Alexander, J. F., & Turner, C. W. (1991). Do reattributions reduce blame? *Journal of Family Psychology, 5,* 192-203.

Mrazek, P. J., & Haggerty, R. J. (Eds.). (1994). *Reducing risks for mental disorders: Frontiers of preventive intervention research.* Washington, DC: National Academy Press.

Newberry, A. M., Alexander, J. F., & Turner, C. W. (1991). Gender as a process variable in family therapy. *Journal of Family Psychology, 5,* 158-175.

Newcomb, M. D., & Bentler, P. M. (1988). *Consequences of adolescent drug use: Impact on the lives of young adults.* Newbury Park, CA: Sage.

O'Donnell, C. R. (1992). The interplay of theory and practice in delinquency prevention: From behavior modification to activity settings. In J. McCord & R. E. Tremblay (Eds.), *Preventing antisocial behavior* (pp. 209-232). New York: Guilford.

O'Donnell, C. R., Lygate, T., & Fo, W. S. O. (1979). The buddy system: Review and follow-up. *Child Behavior Therapy, 1,* 161-169.

Offord, D. R. (1982). Family backgrounds of male and female delinquents. In J. Gunn & D. P. Farrington (Eds.), *Abnormal offenders: Delinquency and the criminal justice system.* Chichester, UK: Wiley.

Offord, D. R., Boyle, M. H., & Racine, Y. A. (1991). The epidemiology of antisocial behavior. In D. J. Pepler & K. H. Rubin (Eds.), *The development and treatment of childhood aggression* (pp. 31-54). Hillsdale, NJ: Lawrence Erlbaum.

Olds, D. L. (1988). The prenatal/early infancy project. In R. H. Price, E. L. Cowen, R. P. Lorion, & J. Ramos-McKay (Eds.), *14 ounces of prevention: A casebook for practitioners* (pp. 9-23). Washington, DC: American Psychological Association.

Olweus, D. (1979). Stability of aggressive reaction patterns in males: A review. *Psychological Bulletin, 86,* 852-875.

Olweus, D. (1991). Bully/victim problems among school children: Basic facts and effects of a school based intervention program. In D. J. Pepler & K. H. Rubin (Eds.), *The development and treatment of childhood aggression* (pp. 411-448). Hillsdale, NJ: Lawrence Erlbaum.

Olweus, D., Mattsson, A., Schalling, D., & Low, H. (1980). Testosterone, aggression, physical, and personality dimensions in normal adolescent males. *Psychosomatic Medicine, 42,* 253-269.

Patterson, G. R. (1982). *Coercive family process.* Eugene, OR: Castalia.

Patterson, G. R. (1992). Developmental changes in antisocial behavior. In R. D. Peters, R. J. McMahon, & V. L. Quinsey (Eds.), *Aggression and violence throughout the life span* (pp. 52-82). Newbury Park, CA: Sage.

Patterson, G. R., Capaldi, D., & Bank, L. (1991). An early starter model for predicting delinquency. In D. J. Pepler & K. H. Rubin (Eds.), *The development and treatment of childhood aggression* (pp. 139-168). Hillsdale, NJ: Lawrence Erlbaum.

Patterson, G. R., & Chamberlain, P. (1994). A functional analysis of resistance during parent training therapy. *Clinical Psychology: Science and Practice, 1,* 53-70.

Patterson, G. R., DeBaryshe, B. D., & Ramsey, E. (1989). A developmental perspective on antisocial behavior. *American Psychologist, 44,* 329-335.

Patterson, G. R., Dishion, T. J., & Chamberlain, P. (1993). Outcomes and methodological issues relating to treatment of antisocial children. In T. R. Giles (Ed.), *Handbook of effective psychotherapy* (pp. 43-87). New York: Plenum.

Patterson, G. R., Reid, J. B., & Dishion, T. J. (1992). *Antisocial boys.* Eugene, OR: Castalia.

Pepler, D. J., & Rubin, K. H. (Eds.). (1991). *The development and treatment of childhood aggression.* Hillsdale, NJ: Lawrence Erlbaum.

Peters, R. D., McMahon, R. J., & Quinsey, V. L. (Eds.). (1992). *Aggression and violence throughout the life span.* Newbury Park, CA: Sage.

Pierson, D. E. (1988). The Brookline early education project. In R. H. Price, E. L. Cowen, R. P. Lorion, & J. Ramos-McKay (Eds.), *14 ounces of prevention: A casebook for practitioners* (pp. 24-31). Washington, DC: American Psychological Association.

Plomin, R. (1983). Childhood temperament. In B. B. Lahey & A. E. Kazdin (Eds.), *Advances in clinical child psychology* (Vol. 6, pp. 45-92). New York: Plenum.

Plomin, R. (1991). Genetic risk and psychosocial disorders: Links between the normal and abnormal. In M. Rutter & P. Casaer (Eds.), *Biological risk factors for psychosocial disorders* (pp. 101-138). Cambridge, UK: Cambridge University Press.

Powers, E., & Witmer, H. (1951). *An experiment in the prevention of delinquency: The Cambridge-Sommerville Youth Study.* New York: Columbia University Press.

Price, R. H., Cowen, E. L., Lorion, R. P., & Ramos-McKay, J. (Eds.). (1988). *14 ounces of prevention: A casebook for practitioners.* Washington, DC: American Psychological Association.

Provence, S., & Naylor, A. (1983). *Working with disadvantaged parents and children: Scientific issues and practice.* New Haven, CT: Yale University Press.

Quay, H. C. (1993). The psychobiology of undersocialized aggressive conduct disorder: A theoretical perspective. *Development and Psychopathology, 5,* 165-180.

Quinton, D., Rutter, M., & Gulliver, L. (1990). Continuities in psychiatric disorders from childhood to adulthood in the children of psychiatric patients. In L. N. Robins & M. Rutter (Eds.), *Straight and devious pathways from childhood to adulthood* (pp. 259-278). Cambridge: Cambridge University Press.

Rae Grant, N., Thomas, B. H., Offord, D. R., & Boyle, M. H. (1989). Risk, protective factors, and the prevalence of behavioral and emotional disorders in children and adolescents. *Journal of the American Academy of Child and Adolescent Psychiatry, 28,* 262-268.

Reid, J. B. (Ed.). (1978). *A social learning approach to family intervention. Volume 2: Observation in home settings.* Eugene, OR: Castalia.

Reid, J. B., Baldwin, D. V., Patterson, G. R., & Dishion, T. J. (1988). Observations in the assessment of childhood disorders. In M. Rutter, A. H. Tuma, & I. S. Lann (Eds.), *Assessment and diagnosis in child psychopathology* (pp. 156-195). New York: Guilford.

Reiss, D. (1993). *The prevention of mental disorders: A national research agenda.* Washington, DC: National Institutes of Mental Health.

Reitsma-Street, M., Offord, D. R., & Finch, T. (1985). Pairs of same-sexed siblings discordant for antisocial behavior. *British Journal of Psychiatry, 146,* 415-423.

Richters, J. E., & Martinez, P. E. (1993). Violent communities, family choices, and children's chances: An algorithm for improving the odds. *Development and Psychopathology, 5,* 609-627.

Rickel, A. R., & Allen, L. (1987). *Preventing maladjustment from infancy through adolescence.* Newbury Park, CA: Sage.

Robins, L. N. (1966). *Deviant children grown up.* Baltimore: Williams & Wilkins.

Robins, L. N. (1978). Sturdy childhood predictors of adult antisocial behavior: Replications from longitudinal studies. *Psychological Medicine, 8,* 611-622.

Robins, L. N. (1981). Epidemiological approaches to natural history research: Antisocial disorders in children. *Journal of the American Academy of Child Psychiatry, 20,* 566-680.

Robins, L. N. (1991). Conduct disorder. *Journal of Child Psychology and Psychiatry, 32,* 193-212.

Robins, L. N., & Rutter, M. (Eds.). (1990). *Straight and devious pathways from childhood to adulthood.* Cambridge: Cambridge University Press.

Robinson, E. A., Eyberg, S. M., & Ross, A. W. (1980). The standardization of an inventory of child conduct problem behaviors. *Journal of Clinical Child Psychology, 9,* 22-28.

Rogeness, G. A., Javors, M. A., & Pliszka, S. R. (1992). Neurochemistry and child and adolescent psychiatry. *Journal of the American Academy of Child and Adolescent Psychiatry, 31,* 765-781.

Rubin, K. H., Bream, L. A., Rose-Krasnor, L. (1991). Social problem solving and aggression in childhood. In D. J. Pepler & K. H. Rubin (Eds.), *The development and treatment of childhood aggression* (pp. 219-248). Hillsdale, NJ: Lawrence Erlbaum.

Rutter, M. (1981). The city and the child. *American Journal of Orthopsychiatry, 51,* 610-625.

Rutter, M., Birch, H. G., Thomas, A., & Chess, S. (1964). Temperamental characteristics in infancy and the later development of behavioral disorders. *British Journal of Psychiatry, 110,* 651-661.

Rutter, M., & Giller, H. (1983). *Juvenile delinquency: Trends and perspectives.* New York: Penguin.

Rutter, M., Maughan, B., Mortimore, P., & Ouston, J. (1979). *Fifteen thousand hours: Secondary schools and their effects on children.* Cambridge, MA: Harvard University Press.

Rutter, M., Tizard, J., & Whitmore, K. (Eds.). (1970). *Education, health and behaviour.* London: Longmans.

Sanders, M. R., & Dadds, M. R. (1993). *Behavioral family intervention.* Needham Heights, MA: Allyn & Bacon.

Satterfield, J. H., Satterfield, B. T., & Schell, A. M. (1987). Therapeutic interventions to prevent delinquency in hyperactive boys. *Journal of the American Academy of Child and Adolescent Psychiatry, 26,* 56-64.

Schweinhart, L. J., & Weikart, D. P. (1988). The High/Scope Perry preschool program. In R. H. Price, E. L. Cowen, R. P. Lorion, & J. Ramos-McKay (Eds.), *14 ounces of prevention: A casebook for practitioners* (pp. 53-66). Washington, DC: American Psychological Association.

Sears, R. R., Maccoby, E., & Levin, H. (1957). *Patterns of child rearing.* New York: Harper & Row.

Seitz, V., Rosenbaum, L. K., & Apfel, N. H. (1985). Effects of family support intervention: A ten-year follow-up. *Child Development, 56,* 376-391.

Shaffer, D., Vieland, V., Garland, A., Rojas, M., Underwood, M., & Busner, C. (1990). Adolescent suicide attempters: Response to suicide prevention programs. *Journal of the American Medical Association, 264,* 3151-3155.

Shirk, S. R. (Ed.). (1988). *Cognitive development and child psychotherapy.* New York: Plenum.

Shure, M. B. (1992). *I can problem solve (ICPS): An interpersonal cognitive problem solving program.* Champaign, IL: Research Press.

Spivack, G., & Shure, M. B. (1982). The cognition of social adjustment: Interpersonal cognitive problem solving thinking. In B. B. Lahey & A. E. Kazdin (Eds.), *Advances in clinical child psychology* (Vol. 5, pp. 323-372). New York: Plenum.

Stewart, J. T., Myers, W. C., Burket, R. C., & Lyles, W. B. (1990). A review of the psychopharmacology of aggression in children and adolescents. *Journal of the American Academy of Child and Adolescent Psychiatry, 29,* 269-277.

Stice, E., Barrera, M., Jr., & Chassin, L. (1993). Relation of parental support and control to adolescents' externalizing symptomatology and substance use: A longitudinal examination of curvilinear effects. *Journal of Abnormal Child Psychology, 21,* 609-629.

Strasburger, V. C. (1995). *Adolescents and the media: Medical and psychological impact.* Thousand Oaks, CA: Sage.

Sturge, C. (1982). Reading retardation and antisocial behaviour. *Journal of Child Psychology and Psychiatry, 23,* 21-31.

Szapocznik, J., Rio, A., Murray, E., Cohen, R., Scopetta, M., Rivas-Vasquez, A., Hervis, O., Posada, V., & Kurtines, W. (1989). Structural family versus psychodynamic child therapy for problematic Hispanic boys. *Journal of Consulting and Clinical Psychology, 57,* 571-578.

Szatmari, P., Boyle, M., & Offord, D. R. (1989). ADDH and conduct disorder: Degree of diagnostic overlap and differences among correlates. *Journal of the American Academy of Child and Adolescent Psychiatry, 28,* 865-872.

Tremblay, R. E., Masse, B., Perron, D., Leblanc, M., Schwartzman, E., & Ledingham, J. E. (1992). Early disruptive behavior, poor school achievement, delinquent behavior, and delinquent personality: Longitudinal analyses. *Journal of Consulting and Clinical Psychology, 60,* 64-72.

United States Congress, Office of Technology Assessment. (1991). *Adolescent health* (OTA-H-468). Washington, DC: Government Printing Office.

Wadsworth, M. (1979). *Roots of delinquency: Infancy, adolescence and crime.* New York: Barnes & Noble.

Wahler, R. G., & Dumas, J. E. (1986). Maintenance factors in coercive mother-child interactions: The compliance and predictability hypotheses. *Journal of Applied Behavior Analysis, 19,* 13-22.

Webster-Stratton, C. (1985). Predictors of treatment outcome in parent training for conduct disordered children. *Behavior Therapy, 16,* 223-243.

Webster-Stratton, C. (1994). Advancing videotape parent training: A comparison study. *Journal of Consulting and Clinical Psychology, 62,* 583-593.

Webster-Stratton, C., Hollinsworth, T., & Kolpacoff, M. (1989). The long-term effectiveness and clinical significance of three cost-effective training programs for families with conduct-problem children. *Journal of Consulting and Clinical Psychology, 57,* 550-553.

Weikart, D. P., & Schweinhart, L. J. (1987). The High/Scope Cognitively Oriented Curriculum in early education. In J. L. Roopnarine & J. E. Johnson (Eds.), *Approaches to early childhood education* (pp. 253-268). Columbus, OH: Charles E. Merrill.

Weikart, D., & Schweinhart, L. J. (1992). High/Scope preschool program outcomes. In J. McCord & R. E. Tremblay (Eds.), *Preventing antisocial behavior* (pp. 67-86). New York: Guilford.

Weissberg, R. P., Caplan, M., & Harwood, R. L. (1991). Promoting competent young people in competence-enhancing environments: A systems-based perspective on primary prevention. *Journal of Consulting and Clinical Psychology, 59,* 830-841.

Weisz, J. R., Walter, B. R., Weiss, B., Fernandez, G. A., & Mikow, V. A. (1990). Arrests among emotionally disturbed violent and assaultive individuals following minimal versus lengthy intervention through North Carolina's Willie M. Program. *Journal of Consulting and Psychology, 58,* 720-728.

Wenar, C. (1984). Commentary: Progress and problems in the cognitive approach to clinical child psychology. *Journal of Consulting and Clinical Psychology, 52,* 57-62.

Werner, E. E., & Smith, R. S. (1982). *Vulnerable, but invincible: A longitudinal study of resilient children and youth.* New York: McGraw-Hill.

Werner, E. E., & Smith, R. S. (1992). *Overcoming the odds: High risk children from birth to adulthood.* Ithaca, New York: Cornell University Press.

West, D. J. (1982). *Delinquency: Its roots, careers and prospects.* Cambridge, MA: Harvard University Press.

West, M. O., & Prinz, R. J. (1987). Parental alcoholism and childhood psychopathology. *Psychological Bulletin, 102,* 203-218.

Widom, C. S. (1989). Does violence beget violence? A critical examination of the literature. *Psychological Bulletin, 106,* 3-28.

Williams, J. R., & Gold, M. (1972). From delinquent behavior to official delinquency. *Social Problems, 20,* 209-229.

Wilson, H. (1980). Parental supervision: A neglected aspect of delinquency. *British Journal of Criminology, 20,* 203-235.

Wolfgang, M. E., Figlio, R., & Sellin, T. (1972). *Delinquency in a birth cohort.* Chicago: University of Chicago Press.

Wolkind, S., & Rutter, M. (1973). Children who have been "in care"—An epidemiological study. *Journal of Child Psychology and Psychiatry, 14,* 97—105.

World Health Organization. (1992). *International classification of diseases (ICD-10).* Geneva: Author.

Yoshikawa, H. (1994). Prevention as cumulative protection: Effects of early family support and education on chronic delinquency and its risks. *Psychological Bulletin, 115,* 28-54.

Zigler, E., Taussig, C., & Black, K. (1992). Early childhood intervention: A promising preventative for juvenile delinquency. *American Psychologist, 47,* 997-1006.

Zill, N., & Schoenborn, C. A. (1990, November). *Developmental, learning, and emotional problems: Health of our nation's children, United States 1988.* Advance Data: National Center for Health Statistics, Number 190.

Zoccolillo, M. (1992). Co-occurrence of conduct disorder and its adult outcomes with depressive and anxiety disorders: A review. *Journal of the American Academy of Child and Adolescent Psychiatry, 31,* 547-556.

Zoccolillo, M. (1993). Gender and the development of conduct disorder. *Development and Psychopathology, 5,* 65-78.

AUTHOR INDEX

SUBJECT INDEX

ABOUT THE AUTHOR

Alan E. Kazdin, Ph.D., is Professor of Psychology at Yale University. He is also Professor in the Child Study Center (Child Psychiatry) at the School of Medicine and Director of the Yale Child Conduct Clinic, an outpatient treatment service for children with aggressive and antisocial behavior. He received his Ph.D. in clinical psychology from Northwestern University (1970). Prior to coming to Yale, he was on the faculty of the Pennsylvania State University and the University of Pittsburgh School of Medicine. Dr. Kazdin has been a fellow of the Center for Advanced Study in the Behavioral Sciences, President of the Association for Advancement of Behavior Therapy, recipient of the Award for Distinguished Scientific Contribution to Clinical Psychology, and editor of various journals (*Journal of Consulting and Clinical Psychology, Behavior Therapy,* and *Psychological Assessment*). Currently he is editor of *Clinical Psychology: Science and Practice* and of the Sage Book Series on Developmental Clinical Psychology and Psychiatry. He is a Diplomate of the American Board of Professional Psychology and Fellow of the American Psychological Association. He has written, co-authored, or coedited more than 30 books. Some of the recent titles include *Child Psychotherapy: Developing and Identifying Effective Treatments* (Allyn & Bacon); *Treatment of Antisocial Behavior in Children and Adolescents* (Brooks/Cole); *Research Design in Clinical Psychology* (Allyn & Bacon); *Methodological Issues and Strategies in Clinical Research* (American Psychological Association); *Cognitive and Behavioral Interventions: An Empirical Approach to Mental Health Problems* (with L. Craighead, W. E. Craighead, & M. Mahoney; Allyn & Bacon); and *The Clinical Psychology Handbook* (with A. S. Bellack & M. Hersen; Pergamon).